The Story

of

SIGIRIYA

SENANI PONNAMPERUMA

Third Edition

ISBN-13: 978-0987345172

Cover Image: This image has been partially restored to convey the splendor of the original frescoes.

DEDICATION

To my children Trishan and Ashani.
Be enlightened.

PREFACE

I first visited Sigiriya as a young boy. At that time, it was a rather forlorn place, indeed. My sisters and I arrived there from the hill-capital of Kandy after an arduous journey in an old car. We were greeted by a group of local guides, a lean and hungry-looking lot at that, keen to pounce on the rare traveler who ventured by. The site was deserted. Running up and down the massive staircases and clambering over ruins, we pretty much had the entire site to ourselves. Much has changed since then.

Over the ensuing years, my fascination with Sigiriya never abated. My interest was rekindled in 2006 when I took my young family on a grand tour of their ancestral homeland. Wanting it to be a cultural experience, I set about collecting information on the subject. Unfortunately, my research proved unfulfilling. While there was a copious amount of information about Sigiriya, it was narrowly sourced and, in some instances, just plain fanciful. Professional works were, on the other hand, far too technical for the average layman to comprehend.

"I should write a book about Sigiriya," I mused. My children challenged me to do just that.

This book has been nearly six years in gestation. It is the result of extensive research and analysis. Numerous assertions have been checked and rechecked. Many of these were discarded when they failed the rigors of critical scrutiny or could not be substantiated by secondary sources. In some instances, I retraced facts to their original sources. For example, I found a copy of *Eleven Years in Ceylon,* published by Jonathan Forbes, in which he described firsthand his rediscovery of Sigiriya in 1831 and included one of the few available sources of the original translations of the Mahavamsa by George Turnour. I also tracked down a copy of the *Journal of the Royal Asiatic Society* published in 1875, in which Rhys Davids describes Sigiriya. I even located an original copy of the *Harmsworth Magazine* published in 1899 in a bookshop in England. As the book progressed, new facts came to light in the most serendipitous ways and were incorporated into the developing manuscript.

As I worked on this project, I was astounded by the sheer enormity of Kasyapa's accomplishment. For example, using only manual labor and rudimentary tools, in just four or so years, hundreds of thousands of tons of raw material were transported up an almost vertical rock face to the summit of Sigiriya rock. There a massive palace complex with gardens, residences, pavilions, and ponds was built. Or consider the frescoes. They once covered a 2,600 square meter section of the western surface of the rock. The detail on the few that remain today is incredible: the ruffles of a skirt, the design in the fabric of a headdress, and anatomical characteristics. They are all faithfully captured in vivid detail.

There is no contemporary account of Sigiriya or the players in its story. But theirs is such a fascinating story and needs to be told. In order to make their story complete, I had to rely on the technique of interpolation—in other words, using known facts to fill in the gaps to reconstruct our narrative. A good example of this is establishing what attire was worn at this time. Determining what was worn by the women in the king's court was not difficult. They are clearly visible in the Sigiriya frescoes.

But what did Kasyapa, the king who spurred the construction of this beautiful citadel, himself wear? In order to determine his attire, I had to rely on the clothing depicted on a statue found at the remote Muhudu Maha Vihara, built by Kayapas's father, near Arugam Bay in eastern Sri Lanka. The figure is of a royal personage giving homage to the Buddha. This attire was reaffirmed by a sixth-century statue in Weligama in southern Sri Lanka. Therefore, it is reasonable to deduce that the clothing worn by Kasyapa during approximately the same time would have been similar.

This book puts forward many new ideas, challenges some existing ones, and debunks others. It reinterprets the evidence in a clear and concise manner but never intentionally veers from the facts. It attempts to visualize Kasyapa's Sigiriya and how he would most likely have liked his story told.

The book consists of two parts. Part 1 provides the background of Kasyapa, describes how Sigiriya was built, explains what became of Kasyapa and Sigiriya, and describes its rediscovery some thousand two hundred years later. Part 2 describes the site as it exists today and provides interesting insights into the many artifacts found there. Additional information, such as how the frescoes were painted and the role of the royal *orodha* (ladies of the royal household–harem) are in the Appendices.

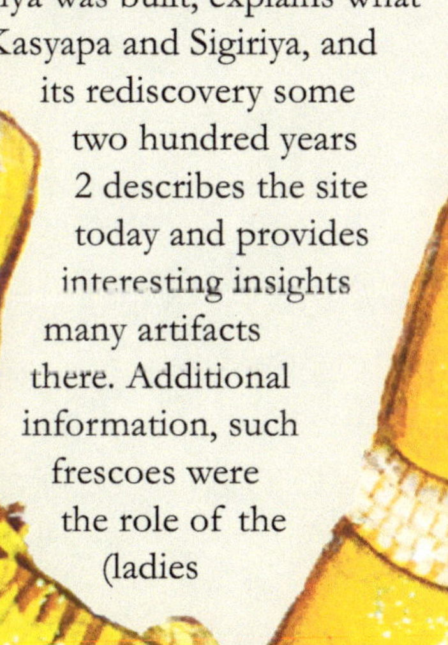

I hope you get as much joy as I have in learning of a great and tragic king of a great and ancient land.

Senani Ponnamperuma
27h September 2017

CONTENTS

"He betook himself through fear to Sīhāgiri
which is difficult to ascent for human beings.
He cleared roundabout, surrounded it with a wall
and built a staircase in the form of a lion...
Then he built there a fine palace, worthy to behold,
like another Alakamanda,
and dwelt there like the god Kuvera."

Culavamsa Ch 39 Ver 2-4

PART 1 – THE STORY

INTRODUCTION

The brooding monolith of Sigiriya looms majestically two hundred meters above the surrounding plains of north-central Sri Lanka. Its history is steeped in tales of cruelty, intrigue, patricide, vision, grandeur, betrayal, chivalry, and abandonment.

In the mid-fifth century, it burst briefly into prominence when, in a mere fourteen or so years, a vast metropolis sprung up around it. Lavish gardens were laid out, and hundreds of thousands of tons of building material was transported two hundred meters up its sheer cliff face to build a magnificent palace, a celestial abode in the sky, worthy of a god-king. Great works of art and theater flourished there. Then, as quickly as it appeared, it disappeared, all but forgotten, relegated to an obscure footnote in history.

The true story of its builder, Kasyapa I (ruled 478–496 AD), is a confusing one, obscured by the mists of time, devalued by omission, and tainted by prejudice. Dealt a cruel hand by fate because of his lowly birth, he was denied a crown, branded a patricide, scorned by the religious establishments, and riled by a great chronicle. Nevertheless, in just a few short years, Kasyapa left to history an enduring legacy of tragedy, exquisite works of art, monumental feats of engineering, and unsurpassed splendor.

We learn of Kasyapa through the ruins at Sigiriya and a brief narrative in the *Mahavamsa*, the oldest and longest authenticated chronicle of any nation's history. This chronicle consists of two parts. The older, referred to as the *Mahavamsa*, was initially commissioned by King Dhatusena, Kasyapa's father, and written by Kasyapa's grand-uncle, the scholar-monk Mahanama. Work ceased on the *Mahavamsa* with the death of King Dhatusena. The second part of the chronicle, known as the *Culavamsa*, was commenced in the thirteenth century, nearly eight hundred years later. It contains the story of Kasyapa and Sigiriya.

From a historical perspective, at about the time the story of Sigiriya was unfolding in Sri Lanka, the Vandals sacked Rome; in India, an erotic compendium known as the *Kama Sutra* was being written; in China, Buddhism was taking root; and in Mexico, the city of Chichén Itzá was being founded.

Most of the rest of the world lay in cultural slumber.

MAHAVAMSA

We learn of Kasyapa and Sigiriya from the Great Chronicle, the *Mahavamsa*. If not for this document, the story of Sigiriya may have been lost forever. There are no inscriptions, cornerstones, or any other records of its construction.

The *Mahavamsa* was written in Pali, an extinct Indo-Aryan language, by scholarly Buddhist monks of the great monastery known as the Mahavihara. Spanning a period of over two thousand five hundred years, it is the oldest and longest authenticated chronicle of any country's history in the world. It is an epic poem glorifying the Buddhist faith, the good deeds of kings, epic battles, invasions, court intrigues, and great construction projects. While intended as one continuous history, it consists of two distinct parts, written eight hundred years apart. The first part, consisting of thirty-eight chapters, is usually referred to today as the *Mahavamsa* (*Great Chronicle*). It covers the period from the arrival of the first Indo-Aryans to Sri Lanka in 483 BC to the death of King Mahasena in 362 AD. It was compiled in about 475 AD by the monk Mahanama, the uncle of King Dhatusena, and the grand-uncle of Kasyapa, Moggallana, and Migara, all key players in our story of Sigiriya. The *Mahavamsa* was first translated by George Turnour, a British civil servant, in 1837. Excerpts of it were first published in a book by a British army officer named Jonathan Forbes. They, too, play cameo roles in our story. The *Culavamsa* (*Lesser Chronicle*) was commenced in the thirteenth century and is a work of many authors. It continues the history of the island, including that of Sigiriya, concluding in 1815, when the island was conquered by the British. We are fortunate that these documents survived the mass destruction of monasteries over the ensuing centuries.

The *Mahavamsa* was written in books referred to as puskola potha. The paper was made from the young leaves of the talipot palm (*Corypha umbraculifera Linn*). Leaves of suitable size, texture, and maturity were plucked and boiled to render them malleable. These were then dried, the writing surface smoothened with a polishing stone, and the paper trimmed to size. Two holes were drilled through the paper using a red-hot wire, and a cord passed through them to hold the individual pages together. The cord was then fastened to two cover boards. Letters were engraved onto the surface with a needlelike stylus. On the completion of each page, carbon black or charcoal powder was rubbed over the page and into the incisions with a rag soaked in resinous oil. The excess was removed, leaving the black powder embedded in the incisions and the writing clearly visible to the reader.

By the early 1800s, the existence of the *Mahavamsa* was known to only a handful of Buddhist monks. A few copies lay forgotten in monasteries scattered across the island. The Pali language, too, was nearly extinct, its idiom known to only a few aging priests. In 1826, a young British government agent named George Turnour was working in Ratnapura, where he developed a keen interest in the local languages of the island. He was especially fascinated with ancient Pali literature.

Having obtained a copy of the *Mahavamsa* from his tutor, Turnour spent countless months poring over the document. Like so many before him, he found it totally unintelligible. Its authors, it seemed, had written a poem without rhyme – mystical, verbose, and incomprehensible.

On one fateful morning of that year, he was approached by the provincial chief priest with a secret he felt could be entrusted with Turnour. The priest said to him, "There is a *tika*—a prose key that would unlock the mysteries of these documents."

A tika is a key, which, when fitted into the mystical verse, reveals its underlying common-sense narrative. Additionally, tikas are usually accompanied by explanatory notes written by subsequent authors. An extensive search was carried out throughout the island, and the missing tika was finally located in the two-thousand-year-old Mulkirigala rock temple near Tangalle, to the extreme south of the country. When Turnour presented the tika to the chief priests of the land, they were dumbfounded. None knew of it. With the tika in hand, the incomprehensible flowery prose of these ancient documents unfolded to reveal their simple narrative of the two-thousand-five-hundred-year-old history of an ancient land and its people.

Another translation into German was done by Wilhelm Geiger in 1912. This was subsequently translated from German into English by Mabel Haynes Bode. This version of the Mahavamsa is considered more authoritative than Turnour's and is now most commonly used.

It is important to keep in mind that the *Mahavamsa* and *Culavamsa* were written by Buddhist monks. Their information came predominantly from monastic sources, and their focus was ecclesiastical. Kings who supported the faith, the Sangha, and its establishments are well represented. Those who were less generous received scant coverage. The monks had their favorite monarchs and, of course, those whom they detested. These biases and prejudices are sometimes mirrored in their interpretation of events. What the Mahavamsa says is just as important as what it omits. For example, the story of King Kasyapa and the construction of Sigiriya are barely mentioned. Wilhelm Geiger wrote in *The Indian Historical Quarterly* in 1930:

> There are a good number of fables, legends and tales of marvels in the *Mahavamsa*, and we must in each particular case attempt to find out whether there is in the narrative a historical kernel or not…All these facts are told in the *Mahavamsa* in a sober and reliable form. We must not forget, however, that the *Mahavamsa* is not a dry chronicle in the modern sense of the word, but a poem. In a poem, embellishments and sometimes also exaggerations may occur. But within these limits I have the strong impression, and whoever reads the *Mahavamsa* without prejudice will have the same, that the author at least wished to tell the truth. He is perhaps sometimes misled by his education and by his conviction, on account of his priestly mode of viewing things, but he never tells a falsehood intentionally.

KASYAPA

The Sigiriya story begins in 432 AD. The Anuradhapura Kingdom in north-central Sri Lanka had by now been in existence for nearly a thousand years. An ingenious and extensive system of irrigation works had made an arid land bountiful. Its capital, Anuradhapura, was one of the largest and most resplendent cities in the ancient world. Gigantic gleaming white stupas such as Ruwanwelisaya, constructed in 90 BC, were the largest brick structures ever built, their size surpassed only by the Pyramids in Egypt. Faxian, a Chinese chronicler who visited Anuradhapura in 411 AD, reported that it had well-maintained streets, multi-storied buildings, richly adorned houses, oil-lamp-lit streets, ponds, baths and parks, piped underground water, and an efficient sewerage system using recycled water.

But this was not a happy time. Misfortune had befallen the land and its people. In 433 AD, foreigners, led by a chieftain named Pandu, had seized control of the kingdom. The land lay under foreign subjugation, its religion defiled, its temples plundered, its great irrigation works neglected, and its people demoralized.

Out in the wilderness, however, there was hope. Resistance to the invaders was coalescing around an inspirational young prince named Dhatusena. Dhatusena was a member of the Moriya clan, a dynastic family who had fled Anuradhapura many generations earlier "for fear of the gatekeeper Subha," who had attempted to exterminate all contenders to the throne. They now lived in a small hamlet close to present-day Polonnaruwa. Unbeknownst to Pandu, the young Dhatusena was living right under his nose at the Dighasandana parivena, a monastic compound in the Great Monastery known as the *Mahavihara* in Anuradhapura. There he was, being tutored for the priesthood by his uncle, the monk Mahanama.

The *Culavamsa* tells us that many good omens foretold of his coming greatness. It tells us, for example, that once, while reciting sacred texts under a tree, it began to rain. A snake, seeing this, encircled him and protected the book and the young boy with its hood; his uncle, the learned monk Mahanama, saw this. On another occasion, a fellow pupil threw

Reconstructed in the 1970s the Ruwanwelisaya is now shorter than the original structure.

animal dung at Dhatusena in an attempt to distract him from his meditation, but Dhatusena was not perturbed. His uncle noted this, too, and thought to himself, "This child is especially gifted; he no doubt is destined to be king and must be protected." Fearful for the safety of this gifted child, Mahanama moved with him to a vihara (monastery) farther away from the capital. But soon, Pandu caught wind of this and attempted to have the young Dhatusena assassinated. Fortunately, having been forewarned in a dream, Mahanama fled with the young Dhatusena deep into the forest just moments before assassins arrived at their abode to finish off the young Dhatusena. For many years, the master and his pupil wandered from place to place and dwelled in the forests as ascetic monks. In these years, Mahanama tutored his young protégé on the virtues of righteousness, kingship, and statecraft.

Many years had now passed. Pandu's second son, Khuddaparinda (ruled 441–457 AD), was the ruler of Anuradhapura. The land groaned under the yoke of foreign subjugation.

Dhatusena had now grown into a strong young adult. It was time, Mahanama felt, for his protégé to follow his true calling. Inspired by his mentor, Dhatusena discarded the saffron robes of a novice Buddhist monk and donned the garb of a soldier and undertook a grueling guerrilla campaign to rid his country of the foreign interlopers. One after another, he slew their leaders in battle, but the invaders held on tenaciously to their ill-gotten prize, quickly replacing one fallen leader with another, denying Dhatusena a speedy triumph. Finally, in about the tenth year of his campaign, Dhatusena was victorious and restored Sinhala hegemony over the entire island.

King Dhatusena (ruled 460–478 AD) acted decisively. Those nobles who had collaborated with the enemy were deprived of their fiefdoms. To those who had supported his campaign he was magnanimous, rewarding them handsomely with positions of power and wealth. Having cleared the land of the last vestiges of the enemy, he applied himself to peace as diligently as he had previously applied himself to war.

Intent on reversing twenty-seven years of foreign neglect, Dhatusena undertook a major revival of the spiritual, economic, and social fabric of the country. He fiercely cleansed the Buddhist religion and restored it to its former preeminence. He expunged the idolatry of the invaders. He built eighteen new viharas. He repaired and provided endowments to many other temples and monasteries. But Dhatusena had not forgotten the bullying and humiliation he suffered as a child; he made no gifts to the vihara where he had animal dung thrown on him as a child.

He refurbished and re-jeweled many statues of Buddha plundered by the invaders. One of these statues was the Abhiseka Buddha in the Abhayagiri Vihara. He built hospices for the poor and crippled. To guarantee farmers a reliable water supply, he dammed the rivers and built eighteen new reservoirs. The mighty Kala Wewa, a massive reservoir of 2,580 hectares, with a capacity of approximately 125 gigaliters (one-fourth the capacity of Sydney Harbor), was the accomplishment he was most proud of. There was a renaissance in Sinhala culture. The arts, literature, and architecture flourished. Most significantly, Dhatusena was instrumental in the compilation of the Mahavamsa by none other than his mentor and uncle, the scholarly monk Mahanama. Dhatusena's munificence was so extensive that the Culavamsa tells us that it was superfluous even to try to enumerate them all.

The Abhiseka Buddha may have looked similar to this less impressive statue at the Dambulla Vihara today. According to the Culavamsa the flame on top of Buddha's head, carrying the band for the alms bowl slung over his left shoulder, his garment and the mandorla (almond-shaped halo) were made of gold. Dark blue sapphires were used for the hair. The eyes were of costly jewels.

Dhatusena had two sons. Kasyapa, the older son, was born out of a liaison between Dhatusena

and"a woman of unequal birth" during his years as a guerrilla fighter. Moggallana, on the other hand, although much younger, was born of the royal bloodline and, therefore, the rightful heir to the throne. Kasyapa, despite the "illegitimacy" of his birth and lineage, was nonetheless accepted by his father and well respected in the royal court.

The Culavamsa tells us that the king also had a charming daughter who was as "dear to him as his own life." She was married to his nephew, Migara, his sister's son. Dhatusena himself had appointed Migara as senapati, the commander-in-chief of his army, a position that made him worthy of his beloved daughter. But all was not well. We are told that Migara "caused her to be flogged on the thighs with a whip although she had committed no offense." She fled to her father. The king, seeing his daughter's garments stained with blood, was outraged. In a fit of rage, he had Migara's mother, his sister, stripped naked and burned alive in retribution.

The *Culavamsa* is silent on the underlying cause of the king's misdirected wrath. We may deduce, however, that

The Avukana Buddha statue was commissioned by Dhatusena. The monk Mahanama may have resided at a vihara here. (circa 5th century)

Dhatusena would not have acted so capriciously against his own sister unless there was some prior provocation, something for which he felt his sister was in no small part responsible. It is most likely that, as was the custom, Migara's mother lived in the same household with her son and daughter-in-law. It is also possible that the mother-in-law played a large part in inciting disharmony between the couple. There may have been a history of prior violence. Not wishing to widow his daughter, Dhatusena probably took what seemed to him the next most logical course of action. This action was to cost him dearly.

Deeply aggrieved by the gruesome death of his mother, Migara conspired with Kasyapa. He fomented Kasyapa's deeply held grudge of being bypassed as the heir-apparent. The throne was rightfully his, Migara whispered conspiratorially, not his less-competent younger brother's. Slowly, Migara estranged Kasyapa from his father and imbued in him the yearning for the royal *senachatra* (the white parasol symbolic of royal authority). Kasyapa and Migara secretly mobilized support among the many nobles Dhatusena had disenfranchised upon coming to power years earlier.

They captured the king, took possession of the royal *senachatra*, quickly wiped out all opposition, and seized control of the government. The young prince Moggallana, unable to muster sufficient support to challenge Kasyapa, fled to India.

Still vengeful and seeking even more revenge, Migara goaded Kasyapa on: "There are treasures lying in the King's palace, O King, has thy father told it to thee?" he inquired connivingly. "Knowest thou not of his intention, O Monarch? For Moggallana he keeps his wealth." Inflamed by Migara's constant haranguing, Kasyapa sent messenger

A painting of a horse-drawn chariot circa thirteenth century.

after messenger to his father, demanding to know where his treasure was hidden. The stubborn old man, however, remained silent. With each rebuke, Kasyapa's anger and resentment grew more intense, and his demand more shrill. Finally, Dhatusena, acknowledging his impending doom, resolved to visit his mentor and friend Mahanama, purify himself in the waters of the mighty Kala Wewa, and then resign himself to his fate. Appearing to relent, Dhatusena sent word that he was ready to point out the place where the treasure was concealed, and he asked to be taken to the banks of the Kala Wewa. Hungry for total legitimacy by acquiring the royal treasure, Kasyapa gladly agreed. But, intent on amplifying the old king's humiliation, he provided him with a "chariot with a bent axle."

The citizens stood in sullen silence as this sorry procession slowly trundled through the city. The once-mighty monarch stood silently, stripped of his regalia, a bedraggled and frail old man. They, his people, could only watch and lament. The *Culavamsa* reminds us, "Thus good fortune is as fleeting as lightning."

As they headed out of town toward the Kala Wewa, some forty kilometers away, the charioteer was moved to feel great pity for his captive and shared his meager lunch of "parched rice" with the fallen king. The king was deeply moved by this simple act of kindness. He ate the rice and scribbled a note for Moggallana, asking him to make this humble charioteer his trusted gatekeeper, the head of the palace guard, when he regained his throne.

On reaching the site where Mahanama awaited him, the king greeted his old mentor with reverence, and as they had done so many times before in their youth, the mentor and his student sat alone.

What misfortune had befallen them.

The monk ministered to Dhatusena. He reminded him of the key tenet of Buddha's teachings, namely, of life's impermanence. Mahanama encouraged him to seek inner solace and quenched in him the desire to prolong his life. Thus, finding comfort, Dhatusena bathed himself in the Kala Wewa. Emerging from the water purified, he pointed to his friend and then slowly, in a sweeping motion to the shimmering expanse of water before him and said, "O, friends, this is all the treasure that I possess!"

The deeper meaning of Dhatusena's simple entreatment was no doubt lost on those present. Namely, that the wealth of the kingdom lay not in material treasure but on a plentiful water supply for its people's sustenance and on the strength of character of its inhabitants.

On being informed of this rebuke, Kasyapa flew into a rage, thinking, "This king keeps his treasure for his son Moggallana, and as long as he lives, he will estrange the people of the island from me." Livid, he ordered Migara, "Slay my father!"

With relish, Migara exacted his revenge. Dressed in full military regalia, he strutted back and forth before Dhatusena, taunting the old king. Realizing that his end was near and determined not to let this scoundrel sully his mind with animosity, Dhatusena entreated his tormentor, "I have the same feeling toward you as I do for Moggallana." This is indeed an interesting choice of words. Its intent is hard to fathom. Did he mean 'I love you as dearly as I love my son, Mogallana'? It seems, under the circumstances, most provocative and reckless. Migara shook his head scornfully and laughed. Finally tiring of this, he had Dhatusena stripped naked, bound him in heavy chains, fettered him in a niche of his prison cell, and slowly entombed him alive by plastering up the opening with clay.

The *Culavamsa* notes sardonically on karma, the circularity of retribution.

> This King Dhatusena, at the time he was improving the Kala Wewa, observed a priest absorbed in meditation, and not being able to rouse him, he had a clod of earth flung at the holy man's head. His own living entombment was the retribution manifested in this life for that impious act.

Here ends the story of Dhatusena. As with all human beings, he, too, was flawed. Along with his great virtues was his disposition to seek cruel revenge. There is no doubt that there were streaks of megalomania and sadism in this great man, character traits that may have been manifest in the genes of his clan. Kasyapa, Migara, and later Moggallana were to each display many acts of cruelty and piety.

> The Lord of men Dhatusena went thus, after eighteen years, murdered by his son, to the King of the gods.

Kasyapa (ruled 478–496AD), in order to further consolidate his power, then attempted to have his brother, Moggallana, assassinated in India. But this attempt was unsuccessful.

The new ruler inherited a prosperous kingdom. His father's relentless pursuit of building large reservoirs and irrigation projects was by now reaping bountiful harvests. The country was at peace. External trade was booming. Merchants from Rome, Persia, Ethiopia, Yemen, China, and India exchanged their commodities at its ports. Trade contributed heftily to the country's coffers.

Kasyapa, however, was guilt-ridden and remorseful. After all, he had ordered the murder of his own father. Patricide was a cardinal sin in Buddhism. By his act, he had earned himself a rebirth, a reincarnation, in hell. A heinous crime such as this had never before occurred in the nation's long history. The people were sullen and unforgiving. Seeking recompense for his indiscretion, he undertook many meritorious acts, but they were of little avail. The hostility ran so deep that all his good works and lavish gifts were ignored or rejected by the clergy. Failing to gain favor through these acts of repentance and fearing the return of his brother Moggallana, Kasyapa grew more and more fretful. He feared for his safety in the present life, and in true Buddhist fashion, he feared the next life. Casting his mind about, he settled on a radical notion: he would build himself a new capital far away from the rancor and ire of the populace and clergy. There, he hoped to find safety and solace.

Kasyapa turned his back on the magnificent old capital and chose an isolated and unwelcoming place deep in the forests of central Sri Lanka as the site of his new capital. It was a foreboding place indeed, teeming with wild elephants, poisonous snakes, leopards, bears, mosquitoes, hornets, and other vermin. Its most conspicuous feature was an immense black monadnock, a solid shaft of rock. The remnant of a lava plug from a long eroded volcano, it protruded ominously two hundred meters into the air and dwarfed everything around it. We do not know what this place was called before this time. We do know, however, that it had been inhabited sporadically by humans from as early as 3000 BC. At the time of Kasyapa, small groups of ascetic monks lived in caves nearby, as they had done since the third century BC. The area immediately around the rock, however, appears to have been abandoned at the time Kasyapa started his ambitious project there.

It was probably while gazing at this giant monolith that Kasyapa first entertained the notion of himself as a god-king living among the clouds. He ordered his architects to build him an earthly paradise, akin to *Alakamanda*—the city of the gods.

The magnitude of the undertaking and the grandness of his vision were breathtaking. Tens of thousands of workers toiled for four arduous years to ready the new metropolis. At its center was a massive citadel surrounded by two moats and three ramparts. Inside were lavish residences, pavilions, ponds, gardens, and, most strikingly, a magnificent palace atop the gigantic rock, two hundred meters above the surrounding plain. This palace was accessible via a passageway that wound precariously along the vertical cliff face. On a small escarpment referred to as the Plateau of Red Arsenic, he built a massive gatehouse in the form of a brightly colored sphinx-like lion thirty-five meters tall. Through its chest, via an almost perpendicular staircase, was the final ascent to the top. It is this feature that bestowed on this site its name, Sīhāgiri—Lion Mountain. We know it today as Sigiriya.

At the appointed time, Kasyapa, the royal family, the ladies of the harem, his ministers, dignitaries, members of the clergy, and foreign ambassadors journeyed from the old capital to the new. Imagine their excitement as the giant monadnock first came in to view. It appeared to them like a gleaming white apparition floating in the distance, tethered against its will to the earth. But, alas, they had to wait. The ceremony was to take place only at an auspicious time the following day.

A cacophony of sound heralded the great day. The grand procession assembled at the commencement of the broad boulevard leading to the western entrance of the citadel. Leading the procession was a large contingent of musicians, dancers, and banner bearers heralding the arrival of the royal procession.

The citizens craned their necks to see their king. Mounted on his royal elephant, Kasyapa was an imposing figure indeed, fit and full of vigor. He was clean-shaven. His long black hair was collected in a conical bun on top of his head and fixed in place with richly adorned clasps and chains. His upper garment was a tight-fitting, nearly transparent cotton half-blouse with short sleeves buttoned at the back. Its collar, sleeve-ends, and high waistband were embroidered and encrusted with gems.

Around his neck, he wore a heavy gold chain studded with sapphires, rubies, emeralds, coral, and pearls. He wore fine ear ornaments and several rings on his fingers. His lower garment was a paridhana commonly referred to today as a *dhoti*. It was made of the finest lightweight cotton fabric, approximately five meters in length. Wrapped around the hips and thighs, it could be worn full-length, like a skirt, or one end could be brought between the legs and tucked into the waistband to create baggy knee-length trousers, which provided freer movement. Being mounted on his elephant, Kasyapa wore his as knee-length trousers. Around his waist, he wore an embroidered sash with a large bow at the rear. He also wore a braided waist cord with tassels. As was the custom, he wore no footwear.

Kasyapa's mighty elephant was bedecked in the finest livery. It was adorned with jewel-encrusted headbands, belts, and stashes. Its long, well-shaped tusks were capped with golden sheaths studded with jewels. Bells and trinkets hung from its sides. Around its legs, it wore jeweled garters, and on its ankles, it wore silver ankle bells. Its toenails were painted in bright colors. The bells and trinkets made a pleasant jangling sound as it walked.

Seated immediately behind Kasyapa on the elephant was the parasol-bearer, the holder of one of the most significant positions in the king's court. He held aloft the white *senachatra*, the parasol of sovereignty legitimizing Kasyapa's right to kingship.

Immediately behind the royal elephant followed the queen in a brightly lacquered and jeweled palanquin. The curtains were drawn open to see and be seen. She was dressed in exquisite cotton and silk textiles and heavily jeweled, in keeping with the richness of Kasyapa's court. Her ladies-in-waiting accompanied her. The royal princes followed the queen, the princesses preferring to join the ladies of the royal harem, who followed closely behind.

This carving from 1543 depicts a king with his parasol-bearer and a young attendant mounted on an elephant in a procession. It is probably similar to that held by Kasyapa many centuries earlier. This chest was made of ivory, gold, rubies, and sapphires at the court of the king of Kotte, Sri Lanka. It was taken by the Portuguese when they conquered parts of Sri Lanka around this period. Duke Albrecht V of Bavaria acquired the chest later in the same century. It is presently on display at the Munich Residenz in Germany.

The ladies of the harem, a key adornment of the entire festival, were the epitome of high fashion. Happy, carefree, whimsical, and barefoot, they danced along the procession route, the dainty bracelets on their ankles making sweet chimes to amplify their merriment.

They wore pleated, brightly colored, hip-hugging *dhotis* pulled up between the legs and tucked in at the midriff, but pulled down intentionally to expose the navel. At the back, the dhoti was fashioned into a stiff, ridged, fan-tail ruffle that protruded behind like the plumage of a peacock. They appeared to be bare-breasted, but actually, their ample breasts were covered with the finest, almost translucent, cotton blouses. Some wore breast bandages referred to as *thanapatiya*.

Haute Couture

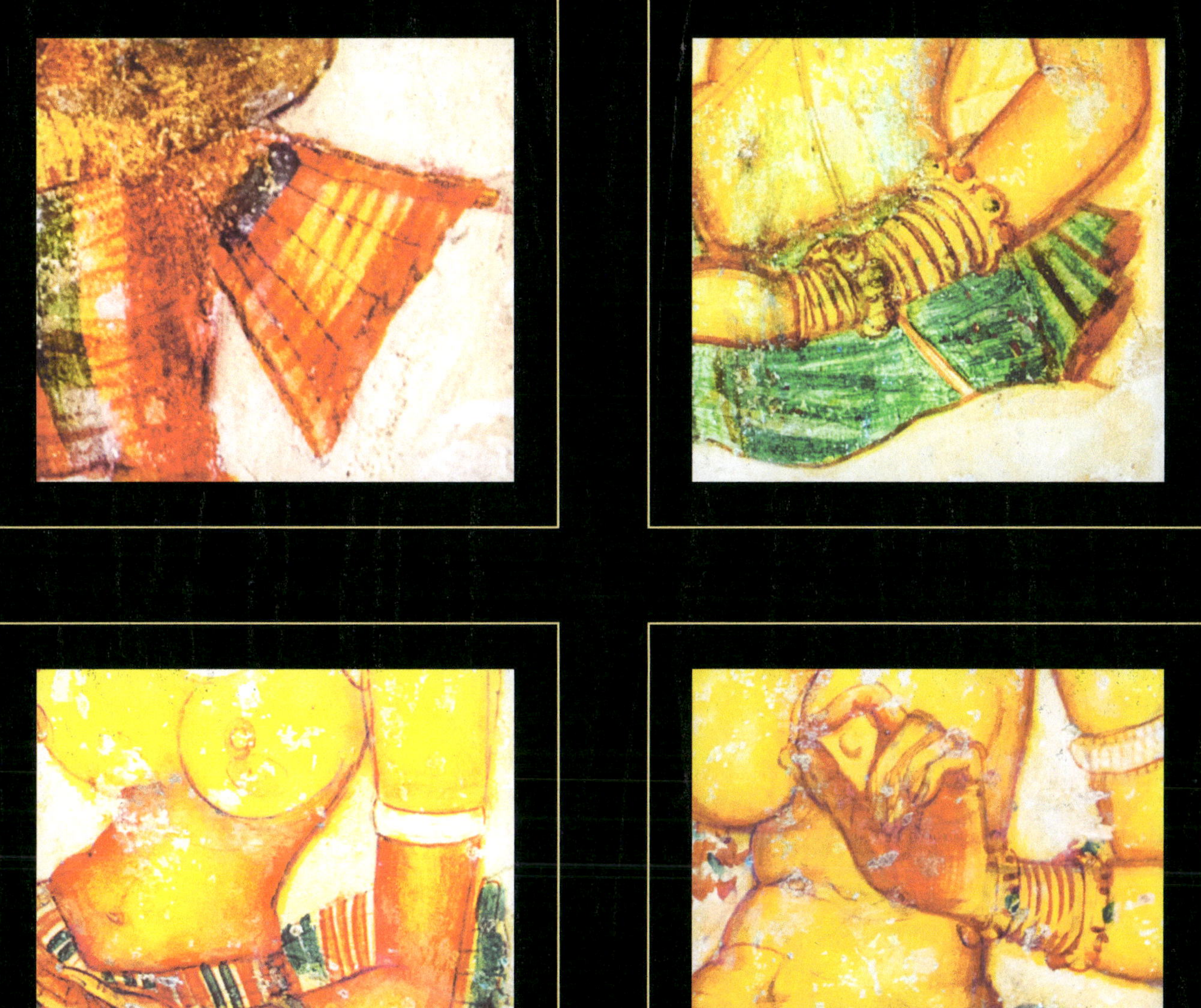

Their hair was styled in the latest fashions atop their heads and intertwined with garlands of flowers. Some wore a tiara, the degree of its embellishment a reflection of their position in the harem. They wore large, heavy gold ear ornaments. Their eyebrows were plucked into thin, elongated arches. Some of the younger ones wore a *bottu*, a drop-shaped mark, on their foreheads and on their upper lips.

They wore red lip rouge on their lower lip but, more interestingly, also had painted or tattooed on their upper lips an exaggerated extension of the upper lip. Around their necks they wore long, thick pearl necklaces and chains with large gem-encrusted pendants. On their wrists they wore thick, multicolored gem-encrusted bracelets. They wore no nail polish. Some had their palms and fingertips stained cinnamon-brown with henna. In their hands they held flowers, which they blissfully tossed toward the awestruck crowd.

Jewels & Adornments

They halted in the vicinity of the middle rampart. Kasyapa dismounted from his elephant, and, at the auspicious time nominated by his soothsayers, proudly escorted his guests over the inner moat, up the flight of narrow steps, and onto the inner rampart where they all assembled. Then, the giant gates of the magnificent, multicolored, multi-tiered gatehouse were theatrically flung open. The guests were agog. It seemed to them as though they had entered paradise. They were awed by the brightly colored buildings and pavilions, set among gardens ablaze with color, cooled by soothing ponds, pools, and streams reflecting a glorious sun. As they gazed skyward, they were spellbound and rubbed their eyes in disbelief. The white apparition they had seen the previous day now appeared as though it were a gigantic wisplike cloud floating just above the treetops, festooned with brightly attired maidens showering flowers on the mortals below. Atop this magic cloud, almost hidden from view, was the gleaming white palace of a god-king, and at its apex was a stupa, its crystal spire emanating shafts of iridescent light that stabbed the noonday sky.

Imagine the foreign dignitaries, entranced by the splendor of the king's court. It was unlike anything they had ever seen in their own lands. Imagine the clergy envious of the great wealth expended for a single individual's personal gratification. Imagine the glee and excitement of the ladies of the harem when they realized that the giant, brightly colored cummerbund girdling the rock was in fact a tapestry, decorated with images of their likenesses. Kasyapa must have grinned mischievously, a glint in his eye, finally feeling proud and vindicated. Unbeknown to them at the time, he had created the most exquisite and enduring example of Sri Lankan art and architecture of all time. It was indeed the creation of a genius. It was the ultimate embodiment of royal power. He had created on earth *Alakamanda*, the city of the gods.

While living in this earthly paradise, Kasyapa continued his acts of piety and repentance. He planted gardens and mango groves throughout his kingdom for the benefit of the common man. In an attempt to legitimize himself, he restored and enlarged the Isurumuniya Vihara, one of the oldest and most iconic monasteries of the land and provided substantial revenue for its upkeep.

Kasyapa then built a magnificent new vihara, incorporated Isurumuniya into it, and renamed the new complex Isuramenu-Bo-Upulvan-Kasubgiri-radmaha, after himself and his two daughters, Bodhi and Uppalavanna. When he tried to hand it over to the clergy, they refused to accept it, fearing disapproval from the populace. Kasyapa tactfully sidestepped this impasse by making a presentation directly to the Buddha. The monks then begrudgingly accepted it as belonging to Buddha. Kasyapa then built another vihara in Niyyanti-uyyana, a park near Sigiriya, and gave this to the Dhammarucika sect of the Abhayagiri monastery. Still haunted by dread for his afterlife, he strictly performed his religious aposaka vows and other religious observances in the hope of salvation.

Migara, too, had concerns about his afterlife. The *Culavamsa* tells us that he built a *parivena*, a residence for monks, which he named after himself. He also built an enclosure to protect the Abhiseka Buddha, the same statue that Dhatusena had restored and bedecked with fine jewels many years earlier. He sought permission from Kasyapa to hold a consecration ceremony for it, one even grander than the one Dhatusena had held. Kasyapa, probably remorseful of Migara's role in his father's death, refused the request. Chafing under this rebuke, the *Culavamsa* tells us that Migara thought to himself, "I shall seek for it again under the sovereignty of the rightful ruler."

Eighteen years had now passed since Kasyapa seized the throne. Moggallana languished in exile in India. He had failed dismally in his grand plan to raise an army to challenge Kasyapa. In this fateful year, however, an intermediary arrived in Moggallana's court, bringing him electrifying news: the commander-in-chief of Kasyapa's army, none other than Migara, had agreed to defect to his side. Gathering up a motley collection of sympathizers, whom the *Culavamsa* refers to euphemistically as "twelve distinguished friends," Moggallana secretly returned to Sri Lanka.

He set up camp at the Kuthari Vihara, near modern-day Kurunegale, nearly a five-day journey from Kasyapa's forces in Anuradhapura and Sigiriya. Here, Moggallana set about assembling a local militia. Kasyapa soon got wind of this development and thought to himself, "I will seize and devour him." He had good reason to be confident. After all, his army was far superior to the ragtag militia Moggallana had assembled. Never a timid man, Kasyapa blithely dismissed the dire warning of his soothsayer, abandoned the safety of his citadel, and set out to annihilate Moggallana.

Kasyapa's army was made up of the *chathurangani sena*, or fourfold army, consisting of an elephant corps, cavalry, chariots, and infantry. The infantry consisted of swordsmen, spearmen, and archers. Mounted on his mighty war elephant, Kasyapa led the charge. Seeing a swamp ahead of him, he turned his elephant to seek an alternate route. Unbeknownst to Kasyapa, Migara, sensing this was the perfect opportunity to put his defection into play, signaled the army to retreat. The shout went out: "Our commander here flees!". The grand army broke and fled in wild disarray.

A war elephant carved on an ivory chest circa 14th century.

Kasyapa remained alone and forsaken.

Flamboyant to the very end, he drew out his jewel-encrusted dagger and placed its cold blade against his jugular, paused for just one moment, and then quickly drew it across his neck, slashing his throat. As his life rapidly ebbed away from him, his eyes rolled lazily in their sockets as he started to lose consciousness, but chivalrous to the very end, he raised the bloodied blade high into the air, sheathed it purposefully, and fell dead.

The royal elephant stood silently, listlessly swaying to and fro, its fine livery tainted crimson with the fallen king's blood. All was quiet now. The wind wafted softly across the tall swamp grass.

Moggallana approached cautiously, wary that this was a ruse, but soon lost all compunction and rushed to his brother's side. He sucked in his breath and gnashed his teeth as he witnessed the carnage. He trembled uncontrollably. His stomach churned. A deep sense of sadness descended over him. His brother was dead.

The moment passed quickly. He braced himself and regained his composure. He straightened himself up and sat tall on his war elephant. A rambunctious cheer filled the air. He, Moggallana, was now king.

Moggallana was relieved and jubilant with the outcome. It had been an easy victory. Kasyapa's suicide also spared him the thankless task of meting out justice against his vanquished brother. In recognition of Kasyapa's act of chivalry and the deep respect Moggallana still held for his older brother, Moggallana cremated him with honor. (The ruin of the stupa at the Pidurangala vihara near Sigiriya is believed to mark the spot where Kasyapa was cremated).

Moggallana (ruled 496–513 AD) returned his capital to Anuradhapura. He meted out severe punishment to those who had supported Kasyapa, putting more than a thousand to death. Lesser transgressors had their ears and noses cut off and were banished. Having spent his anger, Moggallana resorted to being a righteous ruler. When the charioteer presented him with the letter from his father, Moggallana wept, and praised him for his kindness. As was his father's wish, Moggallana appointed the charioteer to the office of gatekeeper. In recognition of his support, Migara remained the commander-in-chief of the army and was granted his wish to carry out a consecration ceremony for the Abhiseka Buddha. Moggallana built many monasteries, including one for his frail uncle Mahanama. His "twelve distinguished friends" were well rewarded with important posts in government.

The Sigiriya complex was stripped of its treasures and gifted to the Dhammarucika sect, who already occupied the Niyyanti-uyyana vihara, built by Kasyapa. Due to the high cost of its upkeep, the general decline of the Anuradhapura Kingdom, and the gradual loss of patronage, it slowly fell into disrepair and was finally abandoned in the thirteenth century. The last historical reference to Sigiriya is in a seventeenth-century poem, the *Mandarampura-Puvata.* It states that King Rajasinha I of Kandy settled some south Indian mystics away from the Buddhist populace in the jungles near Sigiriya. It then slipped into complete oblivion, its past grandeur only reminisced in local folklore.

The *Culavamsa*, written eight centuries after Kasyapa's death, is brief in its description of his reign. Sigiriya is mentioned only twice. Kasyapa is referred to as the "wicked" and "ferocious" Kasyapa. It is obvious that the scribes of the Mahavihara had little love for Kasyapa and his breathtaking secular magnum opus—*Sigiriya.*

In the eyes of these scribes of the Mahavihara, Kasyapa was a low-caste usurper who had ordered the murder of his father, stole the crown, showed little remorse for his heinous deeds, and squandered the wealth of his kingdom on personal gratification and not on the glorification of their religion.

The *Culavamsa's* telling of this story highlights an instance where the authors were in conflict between telling the truth while at the same time expressing their disapproval of Kasyapa. Now, keeping in mind that the Culavamsa would not intentionally spread a falsehood, we need to search for the kernels of truth hidden beneath a veneer of omission, misattribution, poetic license, and hyperbole. A case in point is its narrative of Moggallana's return from India and the battle with Kasyapa.

> The Senapati Migara built a parivena called after himself and a house for the victor Abhiseka. He sought permission to hold a consecration festival for it even greater than that for the stone image of Buddha previously instituted by Dhatusena. As leave was not granted him by Kasyapa, he refrained with the resolve: 'I shall seek for it again under the sovereignty of the rightful ruler'... Now in the eighteenth year the royal hero Moggallana came hither on receiving the information of the Nigganthas, with twelve distinguished friends from India and collected troops at the Kuthari-vihara in the Ambatthakola district.... Moggallana likewise set forth with his army ready for battle, accompanied by his heroic friends.... When the two hosts fell on each other like two seas that have burst their bounds, they fought a mighty battle...

This can be interpreted as "Migara grew dissatisfied with Kasyapa because he was refused permission to perform a consecration festival and decided to betray him. On receiving information that Migara was willing to defect to his side, Moggallana returned from India with a motley collection of friends and set up camp in south-central Sri Lanka. Kasyapa decided to confront him. Moggallana, together with his friends, set out to meet Kasyapa's army. An epic battle ensued."

The epic battle is probably an exaggeration in order to burnish Moggallana's credentials as a great hero. It is most likely that the battle, if it ever took place, was far less monumental. It is more likely that Migara betrayed Kasyapa and was instrumental in the army turning tail and fleeing. Being fully aware of the consequences of defeat, Kasyapa took his own life.

The *Culavamsa* summed up Sigiriya in its entirety with the terse verse:

> He betook himself through fear to Sīhāgiri which is difficult to ascent for human beings. He cleared roundabout, surrounded it with a wall and built a staircase in the form of a lion. Thence it took its name. He collected treasures and kept them there well protected and for the riches kept by him he set guards in different places. Then he built there a fine palace, worthy to behold, like another Alakamanda, and dwelt there like the god Kuvera.

In Buddhist literature, the name Kuvera is associated with the god of wealth, and his city, *Alakamanda*, is the embodiment of all prosperity. Kasyapa and Sigiriya were definitely an embodiment of this notion The *Culavamsa's* association of Sigiriya with *Alakamanda* is in itself a tacit admission that it was indeed a magnificent place. There is some suggestion that Kasyapa was known by the honorific "Maharaja Kasabala Alakapaya" (Kasyapa King of Alakamanda) well before it was used by the *Culavamsa* nearly eight hundred years later. A fifth-century inscription found at Timbirivava confirms this assertion.

It is true that patricide, the murdering one's father, is the first and most heinous crime in Buddhism. And according to the *Culavamsa*, Kasyapa had ordered the murder of his father. Other than this, the *Culavamsa* mentions no other transgression on Kasyapa's part. It can be deduced, therefore, that Kasyapa was a relatively benign and sensitive ruler. Albeit one who did not curry favor with the clergy nor indulge in grand religious construction projects like his father and his brother after him.

The real villain of this sorry saga was Migara, who, with Machiavellian skill, brought about the demise of two kings and his own mother but cleverly evaded earthly retribution himself. If not for Migara's callousness, duplicitousness and deception, Sigiriya may never have been built.

From a historical perspective, Kasyapa's indiscretion of killing his father and usurping the throne had little impact on the overall fabric of society. He displayed a greatness of vision and appreciation of beauty that was unsurpassed by any other king.

Moggallana ruled for eighteen years, carried out many good deeds, and ingratiated himself with the clergy by renovating religious monuments and undertaking other acts of piety. His son committed suicide by jumping into the funeral pyre of his favorite poet. His successor and the one after him were murdered.Two others committed suicide, and two even fled the throne.

The Anuradhapura kingdom survived for another five hundred years, but it was now in terminal decline. It was finally snuffed out by an inglorious defeat to the South Indian armies of Rajaraja in 993 AD.

Kasyapa was the last memorable king of the Anuradhapura Kingdom.

HOW SIGIRIYA WAS BUILT

The *Culavamsa,* the only reliable chronicler of ancient events, summed up Sigiriya in a single short verse. Here was a masterpiece in architecture and one of the grandest building projects of ancient Sri Lanka, yet it received only the scantest mention in the great chronicle. This, however, is understandable. In the eyes of the Buddhist scribes who wrote the *Culavamsa*, the construction of Sigiriya was the gross secular extravagance of a deluded low-caste usurper not worthy of mention. Consequently, their coverage of this accomplishment is reserved. We have no other contemporary account of its construction. However, we can piece together the techniques and materials used by relying on available records for other construction projects from about that time.

Kasyapa was fortunate that he had the resources to realize his dream. He had at his disposal a large, well-trained labor force of hundreds of thousands of workers, craftsmen, and artisans as a result of his father's massive construction projects. As king, he was also entitled to call upon the *rajakariya*, the social compact under which every Sinhalese villager was required to provide forty days of free labor to the king. There is no indication that slave labor was used. Being the monarch of a prosperous and peaceful kingdom, he had the workforce and a substantial revenue base to finance his grand ambition.

The photographs and drawings in this chapter are from the 19th and 20th centuries. They are for illustrative purposes only and are a realistic depiction of what may have been.

Construction of Sigiriya commenced in about the second year of Kasyapa's reign. Most of the trees in the immediate vicinity of the new royal compound were felled. The best timber was set aside for royal residences. Lesser timber was earmarked for other buildings. The rest was burned, and the charcoal transported for use in the iron foundries.

The undergrowth was eliminated with controlled burns, which not only cleared the land but also drove away the wildlife. Particular effort was expended in smoking out the hornets that nested on the cliff face and that were, then as they are now, a menace to all who ventured near.

Tens of thousands of workers were relocated. Hundreds of elephants and teams of oxen were mustered. Extensive brickworks were set up, and the iron foundries at Dehigaha-ala Kanda and the Kiri Oya valley expanded.

Excavations were carried out by swarms of workers, some digging while others carried away the earth in wicker baskets. Earth excavated from the first and second moats were used to build massive earthen ramparts in front of them. Earth excavated from the numerous ponds was used to level out the land and backfilled terraces. Wood from the surrounding forest fueled the massive brickworks and provided charcoal for the iron foundries. These foundries produced case-hardened iron and steel tools, especially chisels, which stonemasons used to work the tough gneiss rock.

Elephants were the bulldozers, tractors, earth compactors, and heavy lifters of the time. Their massive size is deceiving. They are extremely strong, nimble, and dexterous animals capable of lifting up to three hundred kilograms, carrying as much as five hundred kilograms, and dragging logs weighing many tons. They pulled out and pushed down trees, dragged heavy logs, provided brute force for splitting boulders, compacted earth, and pulled heavy carts laden with rock and debris. The huge doorposts for the western gateway, for example, were each fashioned out of a single tree trunk and dragged and put into place with the aid of elephants. Large teams of them were engaged in every aspect of the construction work.

Maintaining a steady food supply for these ponderous beasts was a challenging task in itself. A Sri Lankan elephant, the largest of the Asian elephants, ate up to a hundred and thirty kilograms of fodder a day. Assuming a hundred elephants were on site, that would have been thirteen thousand kilograms of fodder. Supplementing these hefty beasts of burden were large teams of bullocks who, not being as flexible as elephants, were usually harnessed to carts and used in transportation. They hauled bricks, quarry blocks, food, supplies, and fodder for the elephants.

The massive granite boulders on site were either incorporated into the landscaped gardens or demolished. Boulders were split by carving out a groove in the rock and inserting a wedge, which was then pounded into the rock or levered until the rock split. It is most likely that elephants provided the brute force necessary to pull the huge levers that cleaved some of these massive boulders. Rock was quarried in situ. Boulders not part of the grand landscape were chiseled into blocks and used in the construction of the moat and terrace walls. Additional blocks were quarried in surrounding areas and transported on-site by cart.

The building materials of choice were brick and timber. These materials were more versatile and easy to work with than hard granite rock. The timber used for support structures such as uprights and roofing was usually jak. The wood used for doors and windows was satinwood, mahogany, and teak. Timber used for roofing was satinwood or jak. The ax, adze, and chisel were the principal woodworking tools used. Resinous

oils were used as preservatives, and heat was applied to straighten wood. Tongue-and-groove joints with wooden plugs were used, as they enabled solid joints and did not rust. It is highly likely that the woodwork was elaborately engraved, lacquered, and painted. (None of these wooden structures and ornaments survive today.)

Millions of bricks were used in the construction. Clay was extracted from sedimentary deposits from the numerous natural depressions where reservoirs were constructed, and from the excavation of the moats. The actual manufacture took place close to these sources, at numerous small brickworks. The clay was mixed by treading by foot or by cattle. Lean and plastic clay, together with fragments of quartz, were blended to get the correct consistency. The mixture was then set in wooden molds, and the resultant shapes allowed to sun dry. These were then fired in kilns, where the quartz fragments fused with the clay to greatly improve the strength and durability of the brick.

The bricks were transported to the construction site in bullock carts or on the heads of countless laborers. Millions of these bricks were then transported up to the summit of the rock two hundred meters above by forming a line of maybe five hundred or more laborers who stood in a row side by side, in a continuous line from the base of the rock to its summit, handing one brick at a time from one to the other.

The cement used was butter clay. Ancient documents tell us that this was a slurry made of clay, an adhesive made from the resin of the wood apple tree (Feronia elephantum), and coconut water. A very thin layer of this butter clay was applied between each layer of brick. The use of this thin layer of clay meant that each brick was in direct contact with its neighbor and provided stronger compression strength. The brick surfaces were covered with a layer of lime plaster between one and two inches thick and whitewashed.

Terraced gardens and staircases were built to the base of the rock. Then a brick parapet wall nearly two hundred meters long was constructed, which hugged the sheer cliff face as it wound its way around the rock to a plateau on the northeast. Here they built a massive recumbent lion out of brick and wood and painted it in bright and striking colors. A doorway cleverly integrated into its chest led to a near-perpendicular staircase to the summit.

The centerpiece of the new capital was a gleaming white palace complex atop the giant monadnock. Millions of bricks, thousands of tons of mortar, roofing tiles, thousands of pieces of prefabricated doors, windows, and furnishings were hauled up to the mountaintop to build it. There, teams of laborers and craftsmen carried out final assembly. Trees, shrubs, and flowering plants of all sorts were also transported to the top, and exquisite gardens laid out.

A stupa occupied the highest point on the summit. It conveniently served both a religious and practical purpose. The ancient architects had a wealth of knowledge on the impacts of lightning on tall buildings. This experience, gained over a thousand years of constructing massive stupas, was put to good use at Sigiriya. The stupa, with its solid brick core and metal-encased spire, was an excellent lightning conductor and naturally drew away dangerous lightning strikes from the royal residences close by.

Limestone and quartz blocks were used for paving the stairways and passages. Their light color and luminosity complemented the vivid whitewashed walls and were said to glow in the moonlight. Using only human labor, thousands of these blocks, each weighing as much as a hundred and fifty kilograms, were also hauled to the summit. Imagine the grunting and straining as these workmen lugged up these materials through narrow passageways and up steep unfinished stairways. A single

lapse in concentration would have meant losing one's footing and falling to certain death hundreds of meters below.

Wishing to emulate an earthly paradise, they laid out vast gardens that cleverly intertwined man-made geometric forms such as ponds, pathways, and buildings into the natural contours of the land, incorporating rocks, boulders, and the terrain into their grand design. Water, the life-blood of this ancient civilization, was everywhere. Reservoirs, canals, moats, ponds, fountains, and streams were all intricate components of the landscape. The gardens were planted with a multitude of fruiting and flowering plants.

As work progressed, a massive scaffolding was erected against the western and northern rock face. This delicate latticework was assembled from tens of thousands of pieces of bamboo tied together with coir rope. Then, mostly hidden from view, laborers and craftsmen worked on the tour de force of the entire complex. First, they scoured and cleaned the whole rock face, removing all vegetation and loose debris. They then scrubbed the surface clean with water and scourers fashioned from coconuts husks. Then, about a hundred and forty meters above ground, along the entire western and northern rock face, they carved a drip-ledge. This drip-ledge caused water to cascade off the rock face rather than flowing down its contour.

Bamboo scaffolding similar to that which may have been constructed at Sigiriya.

Protected by the drip-ledge, they applied layers of fine plaster. Then slowly, painstakingly, they transformed the virgin plaster surface into the most exquisite example of Sri Lankan art ever created. These were the Sigiriya frescoes (discussed in detail in a later chapter and in Appendix B).

But they weren't finished yet. Then, except for the giant multi-colored cummerbund containing the frescoes, they whitewashed the entire western and northern surface of the rock. They did not find this task daunting. They had prior experience whitewashing large surfaces; after all, they regularly repainted the massive stupas such as the Ruwanwelisaya in Anuradhapura.

Finally, after nearly four years of toil, their work was done. They had created a jewel of Sri Lankan ingenuity for their king.

Alas, their grand enterprise was fully appreciated for only a few short years before it was mostly abandoned and slowly relegated to a dusty footnote in history.

Over the ensuing centuries, Sigiriya became a grim and foreboding place. At dusk, clouds of bats sallied forth from their lairs and into the night sky. During the day, menacing swarms of hornets threatened anyone who came near. Birds built their nests on it. Wild elephants, leopards, and other beasts roamed its disheveled pavilions, ponds, and gardens. The palace in the sky had long ago crumbled and been carried away by the wind. The local inhabitants feared this looming monolith. They believed it was haunted by devils and demons. Few dared venture near it.

For centuries, no human set foot on its summit.

REDISCOVERY

It was now the early 1800s. Nearly one thousand three hundred years had passed since Kasyapa built his city at Sigiriya. The once-proud nation, after centuries of terminal decline, was finally annexed into the British Empire in 1815. With this humiliating defeat, the Sinhala nation-state was extinguished, and the *Culavamsa* ceased to be written.

History, it seemed, had ceased for the great chronicle.

In 1827, a young British army officer named Jonathan Forbes arrived for duty in Sri Lanka and was "immediately attracted to the jungle by the novelty of elephant shooting." Elephant shooting had by now become a sporting pastime of the British Raj. Between 1829 and 1855, more than six thousand elephants, out of an estimated population of thirteen thousand, were captured or shot. (A certain Major Thomas William Rogers of the Ceylon Rifle Regiment proudly boasted that he had single-handedly shot one thousand four hundred elephants before he lost count. He was eventually struck down by lightning and died at age forty-one.) While on one such foray in Ratnapura, Forbes chanced a meeting with George Turnour, a member of the British Colonial Service who was the government agent in the area.

Turnour was a fascinating character, not fully acknowledged for his contribution to our knowledge of Sri Lankan history and for being inspirational in the rediscovery of Sigiriya.

Born in Sri Lanka in 1799 to British parents, he was the grandson of the first Earl of Winterton. He was an idealist, a well-educated man who had joined the Colonial Service not in search of wealth or glory but because of his zest for knowledge and his belief in the betterment of humankind. Turnour's passion was Oriental languages, particularly the unexplored literature of Pali, the extinct religious language of Sri Lanka. He had spent many arduous years unraveling the mystery of the *Mahavamsa*. He, better than any other European at the time, fully appreciated the cultural sophistication of this ancient land.

Forbes spent many days with Turnour and developed a very close friendship with him. He was impressed by the man's intensity and passion. Turnour informed Forbes that the disparaging assertions made by English writers of the time—that the island's people were savages lacking any significant culture or history—were ill-founded. He believed there lay hidden in the jungles of Sri Lanka magnificent lost cities to be discovered. Their discovery would surely dispel these self-inflated notions of Western supremacy.

Forbes recollects in his book *Eleven Years in Ceylon* that, inspired by Turnour's revelation, he set about "to search for those vestiges of antiquity which could further verify the native chronicles." It was not until 1831 that Forbes discovered Sigiriya. He recollects:

We returned from Polannarrua by Minneria and Paecolom; and from thence struck off to the right to search for the ruins of Sigiri, an ancient capital of the island, hitherto unnoticed by Europeans. From Paecolom, after riding four miles, part of our way lying along the embankment, and part in the bed of a large tank, — the morning mist suddenly cleared away, and we found ourselves on the verge of a piece of water, reflecting from its unruffled surface the large forest trees around, with the bare overhanging sides and brushwood-covered summit of the rock of Sigiri, which appeared to have started from the plain, and to frown defiance over the scanty fields and far-extending forests of the surrounding plain.

From the spot where we halted I could distinguish massive stone walls appearing through the trees near the base of the rock, and now felt convinced that this was the very place I was anxious to discover.

Major Forbes goes on to describe how he and his companions ventured through the thick undergrowth and clambered up the dislodged steps of a series of winding stairs that zigzagged up the side of the rock and onto a walled gallery. They proceeded along this gallery for about a hundred meters before, giddy from heat and exhaustion, they were forced to withdraw. Forbes returned in 1833 to continue his exploration of the site, noting that the projecting rock above the galley "had been painted in bright colors."

With its rediscovery, the lost city of Sigiriya soon became a popular exploration site for European adventurers, who recorded their exploits in the many journals and magazines of the time. It was not until 1853 that two intrepid young Englishmen, A. Y. Adams and J. Barley, finally succeeded in climbing to the summit.

In 1875, T. H. B. Blakesley, from the Public Works Department, while viewing the rock through a pair of binoculars, made a startling discovery. To his astonishment, in a protected horizontal pocket about midway up the almost-perpendicular surface of the western side of the rock, he discovered the most vividly colored paintings of what appeared to be naked damsels. We know these today as the Sigiriya frescoes. Much to his disappointment, he was unable to climb to them to view them at close range.

Rhys Davids, for the Ceylon Civil Service, gave a very detailed account of Sigiriya in the *Royal Asiatic Journal* in 1875, and confirmed that he observed the frescoes through a telescope. There is some confusion as to who saw the frescoes first. Since Rhys Davids does not claim he did, it is reasonable to assume that Blakesley saw them first.

Percy Parker, in an article in the *Harmsworth Magazine* in 1899, provides an excellent account of the events that followed. In June 1889, Alick Murray, also of the Public Works Department, finally succeeded in climbing into the "hitherto inaccessible chamber." Murray's recollection of his endeavors is fascinating reading. He describes how the local inhabitants flatly refused to assist him in entering the rock chamber, which they believed was inhabited by devils and demons. No amount of persuasion could make them relent. Unable to get their cooperation, Murray was compelled to import Tamil stonecutters from South India to carry out his work. These stonecutters slowly worked their way up the perpendicular rock, drilling holes into the rock face, and placed iron "jumpers," which they fastened firmly into place with cement. Even these hardy stonecutters had their reservations and were extremely uneasy with their task. At one stage, the key stonecutter downed his tools and refused to go any further. It was only after much cajoling that he agreed to continue, but only after undertaking three days of fasting and praying to his gods for safe passage. When they finally reached the chamber, Murray found that its floor was too steep to get a foothold on. Iron stanchions were set into the floor of this constricted space, and a rickety platform was built on top of it.

Lying on his back on this flimsy gantry, fifty-five meters above ground, Murray worked from sunrise to sunset for over a week tracing thirteen of the frescoes. At times strong winds buffeted his little perch and tore away some of his precious drawings. At other times, irate swallows pecked away at him, resentful of his presence in their domain. Through all this time, the terrified natives watched him from below, expecting at any moment for him to be pounced on by demons and hurled to his death fifty-five meters below.

Finally, when his work was done, Murray decided a memento commemorating his visit ought to be left behind. A bottle was duly obtained, and some newspapers of the day and a few coins were placed inside, and the bottle was then cemented to the chamber.

At this point, seeing that Murray had survived his ordeal and must have scared the demons away, a bold Buddhist priest suggested that a *gatha* (religious chant) for the preservation of the bottle ought to be carried out. Not to be outdone, while the priest was chanting his gatha, Murray and his compatriots, with typical British bravado, rejoined with a hearty rendition of "God Save the Queen."

Murray's tracing of the frescoes stirred considerable interest among the British elite in Sri Lanka. Finally, in 1895, the colonial government instructed Harry Charles Purvis Bell, the first commissioner of archaeology in Ceylon, to commence the full-scale systematic excavation and preservation of the site. Having by now overcome their fear of the rock, the locals volunteered their service so enthusiastically that Bell was never short of willing hands to help him in his endeavor.

An unnamed photographer suspended from a rope trying to photograph the frescoes.

Initially, work was extremely slow, as the thick vegetation around the site was stripped clear. To add to their slow progress, in the very first fortnight, the workers were attacked by swarms of hornets, whose nests hung on the precipitous walls of the rock. Work was delayed while the hornets were smoked out. Then they were confronted with the incessant sun, unbearable heat, and high winds that blew about unpredictably. Bell finally reached the summit using improvised wooden ladders and by cutting six-inch footholds into the rock. This temporary access was soon replaced by stouter iron ladders and a railing. Finally, access to the summit was reasonably safe and slightly less torturous.

Once on the summit, they found it engulfed in a dense canopy of trees and impenetrable undergrowth almost as tall as a man. These were burned off, revealing faint traces of

Mr. Perera on his flimsy gantry. Also visible is the precarious extension on which he perched for many hours. The white lines around the frescoes are from the glue that Murray used to affix his tracing paper to the plaster wall.

ancient buildings buried beneath two to six meters of earth that covered the entire summit. A significant portion of this earth would have been from the stout brick walls that had disintegrated over the years. The whole area was cleared and the debris laboriously scooped up into wicker baskets and tossed over the eastern and southern sides of the rock. Bell was astounded by the true extent of the ruins, which extended to the very edge of the summit, and by the sophistication of its structures.

In tandem with the clearing of the summit, new attempts were made to capture the true vibrancy and color of the frescoes, which Bell felt were lacking in Murray's drawings. The first harebrained attempt to photograph the frescoes was a farcical failure. To do this, they lowered a four-inch-thick hawser from the summit to the ground below and looped it through a hoop in a heavy iron block. A two-inch rope was threaded through the block and then attached to the hawser. A wicker chair was fastened to the hawser and a gallant, if foolhardy, photographer was strapped to the chair and hauled up the side of the rock. Swaying uncontrollably in mid-air nearly fifty-five meters off the ground and fifteen meters from the surface of the rock, the hapless photographer hastily exposed his negatives (they used large photographic plates at this time) and was hauled safely back to Earth. Unfortunately, all his photographs were too blurred to be of any use.

This setback didn't dampen their indomitable spirit. Next, it was Mr. D.A.L. Perera's turn. Perera was the First Draughtsman of the Archeological Survey and worked closely with Bell. Perera courageously set out to do oil paintings of the frescoes while suspended from a rope. After a week swinging in mid-air, exposed to the wind and sun glare, he was taken ill and was forced to spend several weeks recuperating. Undaunted, a platform was built using iron and wooden supports. In this precarious open-air studio, Perera toiled for nineteen weary weeks faithfully reproducing on the canvass the twenty-two frescoes in the chamber. Perera's paintings were displayed prominently in the recently opened National Museum in Colombo and gained the Sigiriya frescoes worldwide acclaim.

Work has continued on the site over the ensuing century. The major effort to date has been focused on the summit and the southwestern part of the royal compound. Large tracts of the royal precinct and the surrounding area still await discovery.

Opposite: The Lion Staircase had not been discovered at the time this photograph was taken. It lay buried in the debris below. The footing grooves for the stairway from the Lion Staircase to the summit are clearly visible.

Above: Excavations of the area above the Large Pond.

EPILOGUE

Sigiriya today is a UNESCO World Heritage site and the most visited historical city in Sri Lanka. It is one of the best-preserved examples of ancient urban planning in the world.

Built by a king tormented by guilt and rejection, it is one of the most vivid and enduring examples of the ingenuity and artistic sophistication of the ancient Sinhalese people. It was the creation of a genius, the ultimate embodiment of royal power. Kasyapa had created a microcosmic paradise on earth—*Alakamanda*, the city of the gods.

His masterpiece was fully appreciated for only the briefest time. Then it slowly fell into disrepair, its decaying splendor still admired by generations of visitors over the ensuring fifteen hundred years. What remains today is a mere shadow of the luxuriant gardens, pavilions, fountains, ponds, paintings, and sculptures which once adorned this place. An audience hall carved out of a rock. A pavilion placed atop a boulder. A giant, brightly colored tapestry encircling an otherwise intimidating monadnock. These were all designed to be one with nature, celebrate beauty and enliven the royal court.

His actions brought him to this place. His vision created it. His destiny forfeited it. His legacy bequeathed it to millions to admire over the ensuing centuries.

We do not know if Kasyapa found solace in the afterlife. We do know, however, that his masterpiece at Sigiriya has now stood for over a half a million days, and brought him immortality.

Lotus growing in a small pond on the summit.

PART 2 – THE SITE

THE CITADEL

It is difficult for a visitor today to comprehend the sheer splendor that was Sigiriya fifteen hundred years ago. It was built, some say, to emulate *Alakamanda*, the city of the gods.

While the ancient capital of Anuradhapura and the medieval capital of Polonnaruwa may eclipse Sigiriya in their size and in the number of their ruins, neither can surpass Sigiriya for its aesthetic elegance, grand vision and ecologically sensitive. It is one of the best preserved examples of ancient urban planning in the world. Unlike other ancient ruins in Sri Lanka, Sigiriya is unique in the secular nature of its architecture. There are no significant religious edifices on the site.

The royal citadel occupied an area about two and a half kilometers in length and one kilometer in width. It was surrounded by two moats and three ramparts. It was designed predominately as a royal residence and not as a fortress. Incorporated into its design were numerous passive defenses that provided a reasonable level of protection. While tactically impregnable and secure, it was strategically vulnerable. An attacker merely had to lay siege and starve out its inhabitants.

The citadel was the private preserve of the royal household. It was a picturesque recreation of paradise, incorporating an idealized version of nature. It was not meant to be seen all at once; but rather as a series of framed compositions of formal and informal styles laid out to present a series of views and tableaus. The wide formal gardens with ponds and pools created illusions of streams flowing through idyllic parks. The walls throughout the complex were given a mirror-like white sheen to generate an impression of spaciousness, and to enhance the perception that this was a magical place. Eye-catching pavilions large and small, halls, gateways, galleries, and towers were festooned throughout the landscape. These lead to winding paths, natural boulders, and slopes that were ingeniously incorporated to create a series of views and tableaus. At the pinnacle of this earthly paradise were the gleaming white rock and the palace atop it.

View of Western Gardens from the summit.

The compound is broken up into two distinct precincts. The Western Precinct, located on the west side of the rock, occupies an area of approximately 56 hectares. The precinct was bisected into the northern and southern sectors by a wide boulevard that led from the main western entrance towards the stairs to the summit. The boulevard was lined with exotic gardens. The gardens commence at the entrance with the symmetrical gardens and lower palaces, which followed an echo plan. That is to say, each side mirrored the other. The royal households spent most of their time in these compounds. It is important to understand that palaces in warmer climates such as in Sri Lanka were not large, enclosed edifices like those found in colder climates. Rather, they were usually a collection of relatively open structures designed to provide good ventilation and cooling and were scattered throughout the royal compound. The mirror-image symmetry of the formal gardens led seamlessly into the natural disarray of the Boulder Gardens and then up through the Terraced Gardens to the foot of the Sigiriya rock. Wide, steep staircases then wound their way to the palace on the summit.

The Eastern Precinct was an area of approximately forty hectares located on the eastern side of the rock. This area is heavily forested and has remained mostly unexplored by archeologists. Recent excavations have revealed a rampart and moat and at least three entrances. Some have suggested that it functioned as a ceremonial area. Other possibilities are that the inner ramparted area was reserved for the royal harem and the outer area occupied by the royal household.

The ruins seen today are less than twenty percent of the structures that once graced the area. Most buildings were made of wood. Consequently, there is very little evidence of these structures. Those built with stone and brick have survived the ravages of time and provide us a rare glimpse of the opulence and grandeur of an ancient era. Many ruins still lay hidden and are yet to be discovered.

Being located in the dry zone of Sri Lanka, with only moderate and seasonal rainfall, Sigiriya's builders employed a sophisticated network of water management. Precious rainwater was harvested and stored at every opportunity and distributed via an intricate system of large reservoirs, streams, channels, and underground pipes to the countless ponds, pools, baths, and other facilities throughout the compound. Some of these waterworks are still functional today. Except for the moats and ramparts, all other defenses were passive in nature and cleverly integrated into the landscape. These included the relatively narrow thoroughfares with buildings straddling them; steep, almost perpendicular stairs; and numerous ponds, terraces, and walls that made elephants and horses ineffective within the compound and provided excellent protection for its inhabitants. It was, however, primarily a royal compound and not a fort.

The Sigiriya Cultural Triangle project is responsible for the archeological site at Sigiriya. It has been their policy to only partially excavate the ruins at Sigiriya, leaving areas unexcavated for future generations. As a result, only the right side of the western precinct has been extensively excavated.

This narrative follows the natural progression of a visitor on entering the precinct at the Western Gate and culminating on the summit with its grand vista below. Give your imagination free rein as we explore a masterpiece.

Next Page: A mural from the Dambulla Cave Temple. Its exact vintage is uncertain but it is from a time much later than Kasyapa. The pavilions depicted in the mural may have looked similar to the far more elaborate ones constructed at Sigiriya. (An interesting aside can be seen through the doorway of the pavilion in the bottom center of the mural).

Ramparts and Moats

The Sigiriya citadel was surrounded by three massive ramparts and two moats. The outermost earthen rampart was forty-three meters wide and over eight kilometers in length. It encircled the entire citadel. The rampart bisected the Sigiri Mahavava, the huge man-made lake located to the south, securing an internal water supply for the moats and residents. The area surrounding the rampart was of a slightly lower elevation and may have been flooded in the event of an attack. The outer moat, traces of which are faintly visible today, was fifty-two meters wide and four meters deep. Access across these moats was via detachable wooden causeways, which could be easily dismantled or destroyed in the event of an attack. The middle rampart was thirty-seven meters wide. An eight-meter-wide roadway ran along its top. This roadway was covered with a tiled roof. The lack of any solid foundations suggests that this was a pillared timber structure. The inner moat was about twenty-three meters wide. While providing an additional layer of protection, its primary purpose was to provide cooling. It was lined with hundreds of thousands of hewn stone blocks set out in terraces. As an extra disincentive to would-be attackers, this moat was stocked with thousands of ravenous crocodiles. A brick wall, two meters thick at its base and three meters high, stood inside this rampart, and a paved stone path ran on top of it. This had a tiled roof. Construction on the outer defenses ceased abruptly when Kasyapa died. This may explain why on the northern and southern sides, there are large outcrops of rock that obstruct the inner moat negating any defensive intentions. Being substantial obstructions, these may have been earmarked for removal later.

Entrances

The Sigiriya citadel had four entrances. The ceremonial entrance was through the western gate, which was reached by crossing the inner moat via a small wooden bridge. A steep, narrow stairway made of quartz-stone, which glowed gently in the moonlight, led to the top of the gleaming white three-tied inner rampart. Visitors then entered an elegant, highly decorated pavilion set on top of the inner rampart.

The holes left by the timber support pillars suggest that it was an ornate brightly-colored multi-storied three-chambered structure made of timber and brick with a tiled roof. The floor of this structure was of marble. The narrow entranceway, stairs, and buildings which straddled the main thoroughfare of this entrance suggest that there was intended for pedestrian traffic only. It is most likely that the royal entourage either walked or was carried in palanquins through this entrance. (A palanquin is a covered litter or chair carried on the shoulders of four men).

The three other entrances were solid structures of stone and brick and could accommodate vehicular traffic. The southern entrance had a sizeable multi-tied entranceway.

Miniature Water Gardens

Just inside the western gate are the Miniature Water Gardens, which were only excavated in the mid-1980s. Each garden is approximately ninety meters long and thirty meters wide on either side of the main boulevard. Only the southern section of this garden has been excavated and reveals that it is very different from the other gardens at Sigiriya. There are five distinct areas in this garden, which once had roofed pavilions, pools, courtyards, fountains, cisterns, and winding waterways. An unusual characteristic of this garden is the use of very shallow marble and pebble-lined pools around the pavilions. Slow-moving water flowed through these pools offering both pleasant aesthetics and a soothing, cooling effect. Being outside the main garden complex, these may have been used to entertain lesser functionaries.

These gardens appear to have been constructed in two phases. The first construction appears to have been in the time of Kasyapa. A subsequent building program appears to have taken place around the tenth and thirteenth centuries at a time when Sigiriya was a Buddhist monastery. This second construction phase may be a reflection of the progressive decline and abandonment of the site, with activity being concentrated towards the main entrance.

Opposite: Visitors to this pavilion washed their feet in the small foot wash which flowed between the steps.

Top: An example of the slow destruction of the site caused by vegetation.

PAVILION GARDENS

The Pavilion Gardens is the oldest surviving example of the charbagh quartered garden plan in the world. It predates similar designs at the Taj Mahal and Jaigarh Fort in India by over a thousand years. The gardens consist of a large walled compound with four massive L-shaped pools and ancillary compounds. At its center is an island linked to the main precinct by four causeways, which once had ornate entrances. At the head of each causeway were massive gateways. The largest of these gateways facing the west had a triple entrance. The holes left by the huge timber doorposts suggest that it was an elaborate multi-story gatehouse of timber and brick with tiered tiled roofs. The pools were lined with brick, plastered, and then highly polished. They were supplied with water via underground pipes from the massive artificial lake to the south and drained into the inner moat to the west. They were also interconnected to each other by pipes and were capable of being filled to different depths. On the central island was a large pavilion with an open lower floor, which straddled the main thoroughfare. It may have had up to two enclosed upper floors. Behind the L-shaped pools are two large rectangular compounds with marble-lined reflecting pools and pavilions set in shallow water. These compounds could also be accessed privately from the bathing pools via corbelled tunnel passageways.

The repeating design, the corbelled tunnels leading to the rear compounds, and large pavilions has led to speculation that this may have been the main recreation area for the king and his harem.

Tradition has it that the ladies of the harem, some speculate they numbered in the hundreds, would leave their clothes in the pavilion and enter the pools naked. Kasyapa would observe them from the upper floors, descending to the pavilion when the ladies emerged from the pool to dry themselves. The king would strike up a conversation with any that took his fancy. The rest would disperse discretely.

The areas beyond these compounds may have contained many wooden buildings. No traces of these structures have been found to date.

Opposite: Corbelled Tunnels lead from each pool to the rear compound.

Top: A natural boulder left in the pool to add character and provide a convenient roosting spot for swimmers.

Above: Decorative brickwork in the Pavilion Gardens.

Fountain Gardens

An interesting feature of the Fountain Gardens is the sudden appearance and disappears of water. Springs appear out of nowhere, and streams seem to disappear into thin air.

The upper level is dominated by two meandering streams, which flowed along its length. These streams were feed by what appear to be natural springs from water supplied to them through sealed underground drains connected to storage tanks further up the garden. The streams have a practical and ingenious design. The bottom surface of each stream is built at two levels. On the outer edge of the streams are narrow brick-lined channels while the upper surfaces are broad and flat. This ensured that during the dry session, water loss was minimized by concentrating it in a deep narrow channel. When water is abundant, the entire stream was filled. These streams appear to terminate suddenly, disappearing into small pits only to reappear again on the lower level.

Water from the upper level reappears through two different outlets and flows into two long deep rectangular pools. The first is by a shallow marble-lined stream that flows over a broad waterfall into the rectangular pool. Water to this stream is supplied by a series of fountains interspersed along its length. The fountainheads are made of circular limestone blocks, each with a water spout drilled in a geometric pattern. The fountains and marble-lined ponds are only functional when there was an ample water supply. No longer being supplied by their original water source, these fountains today only operate during the rainy season when their storage tanks are filled naturally by rainwater. A second is via a set of gentle staggered waterfalls which are supplied directly by underground drains and work independently of the main waterfall. The reason for this layout is to ensure that, even during a drought, there was always a sufficient flow of water through the rectangular pools to prevent them from stagnating. The terraced walls are built of stone blocks with brick facing. All the brickworks were plastered and most likely painted. The partial remnants of wall plaster are still visible, at the near end of the Fountain Gardens, under a crude modern-day shelter made of corrugated iron. The terraces were probably planted with brightly colored flowering plants.

The Meandering Streams on the upper level of the Fountain Gardens appear as though from natural springs. They flow the full length of the upper level and disappear abruptly into pits and reappear on the lower level of the gardens to flow down more formal channels before cascading as waterfalls into two rectangular pools.

Lake Palaces & Gardens

Mostly obscured from view, the Moated Palaces and Gardens are often overlooked by visitors. Located immediately behind the Fountain Gardens, they are the largest gardens by area in the citadel. They consist of rectangular compounds surrounded by high retaining walls. Inside each are two large circular built-up islands surrounded by moats twenty meters wide. Bridges cut or built into the underlying rock provided access across the moats to these islands. The moats were mainly for cooling and aesthetic purposes.

On the flattened surfaces of each island are the Lower Palaces (Sitala Maliga). These may have been the royal residencies; one for the king and his entourage, and the other for the queen and hers.

The Sigiriya rock is clearly visible from these vantage points. Imagine what it would have looked like in the time of Kasyapa. If he looked eastward from his palace, he would have seen the overpowering white rock festooned with colorful frescoes and on its summit his abode in the sky with its glistening copper-colored roof. If Kasyapa were to have looked down into the moat, there too he would have seen the reflection of his magnum opus in the tranquil waters below. Tradition has it that Kasyapa used to stand at the window of his palace and watch his harem and children frolic in the gardens below.

This & Next Page: The once gleaming white rock with its palace and brightly colored frescoes was clearly visible from the Lake Palace. They were also reflected on the waters of the moat as they still are today.

Octagonal Pond and Gardens

The Octagonal Pond is approximately thirty meters in diameter and one hundred and ten meters in circumference. The walls of this pond today are stone-lined. Given the lack of any staircase today it is very probable that it was brick-lined and rendered with white plaster.

This pond is believed to have been used exclusively by the king and his immediate royal court. Before each use it was flushed out into the moat of the northwest Lower Palace and refilled with fresh water. A bathing pavilion was located on the far side of the pond. A drip-ledge from a lean-to roof is all that remains of this. Next to this pond are an octagonal pavilion and a circular structure that appear to have been constructed after Kasyapa's time.

Mirroring the Octagonal Pool on the opposite southern side is a rectangular pool with earthen embankments. It has been suggested that this may be an unfinished construction from a later period.

Many other lesser structures lie to the north and south of those described here.

The eastern boundary of the Octagonal Pool Gardens is marked by the huge inner citadel wall built of granite blocks faced with a thick brick outer cladding. The brick cladding suggests that these walls were plastered too. Some believe it was originally twice its present height.

BOULDER GARDEN

The Boulder Garden along the western side of the rock was intentionally designed to create an illusion of natural harmony and to strike the eye with beautiful organic compositions.

Several boulders have rock shelters beneath them. Most of these shelters were originally constructed by Buddhist atheists from as early as the third century BC. Some contain inscriptions recording the names of patrons who donated them to the local monks. A noticeable feature of these shelters is the presence of drip-ledges, which prevent rainwater from flowing down into the caves. Kasyapa's architects and landscapers cleverly incorporated these caves into their grand design, enhancing and decorating them to provide a surreal environment consistent with a paradise garden. On top of almost every boulder was a pavilion of some sort with tiled roofs. The hollow indentations, visible on these boulders today, are the tell-tale remains of footings incised into the rock for the foundations for these structures.

An immense wall marks the commencement of the inner citadel. It was originally twice its present height. This towering defensive structure consists of several huge retaining walls built of roughly cut stones that were faced with brick and white plaster. Subject to many phases of reconstruction, the original base of this wall now lies many meters below the present ground level. Immediately inside these walls to the right are the remains of a monastery built between the fifth and twelfth centuries.

The organic nature of these gardens can be observed in the way natural features were adopted or enhanced to create functionality. Examples of these are the Cistern Rock, Audience Hall, Cave 7, and numerous other structures scattered about.

Recent excavations in this area have uncovered exquisitely carved figurines made between the seventh and tenth centuries. They are models of the Sigiriya frescoes. These sculptures are unique in that they are representations of secular, non-religious, art designed to be admired as objets d'art. They are believed to have been sold as souvenirs at the time Sigiriya had reverted to a Buddhist monastery.

The main stairway leading up to the Terraced Gardens. The thick brick cladding of the granite block retaining wall is clearly visible. This suggests that these walls too were plastered and possibly decorated with paintings.

This seat was probably part of the furnishing of an anteroom where people waited to be summoned for an audience with the king.

Opposite: Another example of a shelter under a boulder with the ever-present drip ledge. Located by the stairs leading to the summit it was brightly decorated and used as a rest stop for weary climbers.

Above: Consistent with the organic theme, these stairs tunnel between two boulders which may have been plastered and brightly decorated.

This rock shelter has a clearly visible drip-ledge and a number of very faint paintings of female figures. Facing in a northerly direction, they are kneeling and carrying flowers. Painted many centuries after the Sigiriya frescoes, the artist may have drawn his inspiration from them. These paintings are not true frescoes but rather colored line drawing which are sadly lacking in the gracefulness and elegance of the frescoes commissioned by Kasyapa.

Top: This boulder was intentionally split to create the Cistern Rock and Audience Hall. On the higher upright section is a cistern carved into the rock which was feed via an elevated aqueduct. Water from this cistern was used for ritual ablution by visitors before an audience with the king.

Above: The Audience Hall with a five-meter-long royal seat was carved out of the on the lower section of the boulder. The whole area was plastered and painted. (The original plaster is still visible on the seat).

Opposite: The Cobra Hood Cave gets its name from the shape of the boulder under which it is located. This boulder may have been chiseled away to create this profile and work abandoned before it was completed. A Brahmi inscription dated to around the third century BC tells us that it was donated by a chief named Naguli.

Above: The paintings on the ceiling of the Cobra Hood Cave have been dated to around the sixth century and consist of a combination of geometric and spiral motifs.

The Terraced Gardens are fashioned out of the natural hill at the base of the western slope of the Sigiriya rock. Roughly hewn granite blocks were used to build retaining walls with landings that rise in a series of concentric circles one above the other. These had a brick cladding and were plastered. We do not know what purpose this area served. It is most likely that it was planted with exotic trees, shrubs, and flowering plants. In some of the broader areas are the remains of some buildings, but their age is uncertain.

There are two massive brick stairways with limestone paving, which provide access from the Boulder Gardens through the Terraced Gardens to the rock itself. The paths leading to these stairs are possibly the only two which bear some resemblance to the original paths. One of these stairways passes a cave believed to have been a shrine for the goddess Abhrasthita (Aphrodite). The other, via a large archway created by two boulders, also provides access to the terraced gardens above. Both these stairways terminate in a landing located near the middle of the western face of the rock. Beam holes cut into the rock suggest that this landing may once have been covered. The Mirror Wall commences from this landing.

In an area on the north side, presently inaccessible to visitors, are the remains of a third staircase, which leads to the plateau in front of the Lion Staircase. This appears to have been partially built of wood and probably intended for easy destruction in case of an attack.

Opposite: The main stairway from the Boulder Gardens ascends between natural boulders

Above: The main stairway continues to ascend steeply through the Terraced Gardens and zigzags up to the Mirror Wall.

Mirror Wall

The Mirror Wall, now stained in hues of orange, was once a highly polished white masonry wall that wound its way precariously along the near-perpendicular western rock face. Commencing at the top of the stairs at the base of the rock, it traversed a distance of two hundred meters to a small plateau on the northern side of the rock on which the Lion Staircase is found. It is believed that its mirror-like sheen was achieved by using a special plaster made of fine lime, egg whites, and honey. This surface was then buffed to a brilliant luster with beeswax. The wall provided an irresistible tablet, on which are inscribed the musings of many an intrepid traveler. One graffito states that the plaster was so highly polished that it reflected the painting from the opposite rock wall. It is one of the few structures at Sigiriya which has stood almost intact over the fifteen centuries. It is a testament to the ingenuity and workmanship of the ancient craftsman who built it.

The Mirror Wall is actually a parapet wall with a one-and-a-half-meter-wide inner passageway, and its outermost section is built up to create a protective wall. The walkway was paved with polished marble slabs. Only about one hundred meters of this wall exists today, but brick debris and grooves on the rock face along the western side of the rock clearly show where the rest of this wall once stood. The western portion of the wall did not have a roof. Its location, away from the prevailing winds, and the drip ledge above it provided excellent protection. The north-western section, now collapsed, was directly in the path of harsh prevailing wind and rain and was therefore covered with a roof. Holes and grooves chiseled into the rock on the opposite side of the wall were mounting points for supporting beams of a roof. Numerous indentations along the rock face suggest that these were little niches for oil lamps to illuminate the passageway at night, much as nightlights are used today. At the top of the final stairs of the mirror wall passage was a stout doorway, its doorjambs are clearly visible even today. The recent discovery of a painting of a figure, which appears to be that of an apsara, on the exterior of the Mirror Wall suggests that this wall too may have been painted at some point in time. However, this painting has a very strong resemblance to a one found in Cave 7 in the Boulder Gardens, suggesting that it was painted after the time of Kasyapa.

Opposite: Even today, when the light is right, the Mirror Wall still shines justifying its name.

Above: Grooves chiseled into the rock on the opposite side of the wall were mounting points for supporting roof beams. Numerous indentations along the rock face suggest that these were niches for oil lamps to illuminate the passageway at night, much as nightlights are used today.

The Frescoes

Protected in a small, sheltered depression a hundred meters above ground, they float effortlessly among the clouds, bejeweled and radiant, their ample breasts and sinuous bodies barely concealed beneath their translucent gossamer garments. Some say they are celestial nymphs, apsaras, carrying flowers to shower upon kings and heroes below. Others suggest that they are Kasyapa's queens and concubines painted in an ancient picture gallery. They have been the subject of speculation for over fifteen hundred years. Poets, philosophers, archaeologists, and dreamers have pondered their true meaning. They simply smile enigmatically in return.

But who were they? Why were they placed there?

In Hindu and Buddhist mythology, apsaras were beautiful supernatural female beings. They were believed to be the guardians of fallen warriors. Waif-like creatures, they were often depicted full-bodied with legs bent taking flight. They could be compared in some ways to angels.

The females in the Sigiriya frescoes are only depicted three-quarter-length from the hips up. They are neither flying nor dancing. They are not all young, lithesome, or waif-like. They appear full-blooded and alive. Furthermore, there is no Sri Lankan art up to this period depicting apsaras. Even the *Mahavamsa* pays scant attention to them. It is, therefore, unlikely that they were apsaras.

They hold flowers and generally have a north-facing disposition, the direction of the Pidurangala temple about a kilometer away. But they display no solemnity, piety, nor discernible narrative. Perhaps they face northward, in the direction of the climb to the summit, welcoming visitors from below. It is unlikely that they have any religious significance.

The rich adornments, dress, lifelike appearance, vibrant use of color, and the true rendition of facial and anatomical characteristics support the view that the artist drew his inspiration from a more earthly source, namely, the ladies of Kasyapa's harem (Appendix A).

The most telling validation of this view is that each of them wears a dainty black necklace around her neck. Closer scrutiny reveals, however, that it is not a necklace at all, but a delicate three-circled tattoo (see photo). The prominent but unobtrusive display of this tattoo, proudly worn, was meant to clearly identify these ladies as belonging to the king. They were ladies of the king's harem, dressed in their finest. They were to be admired but not touched. For this reason, they were depicted in true form, voluptuous and desirable, but shorn of any earthly sexuality. They were not intended to be titillating.

Depicted as celestial beings showering flowers on those below, apsaras if you like, they are, without doubt, the women of the royal court of Kasyapa. They were intended to evoke a sense of wonderment and to project the opulence and grandeur of Kasyapa, the all-powerful god-king.

They are simply a celebration of beauty.

This lady appears to be in the early stages of pregnancy. She is also the only lady with elongated earlobes caused by the earlobe being stretched by weighty ear ornaments. This suggests that she may have been from South India. The red object on her back is a tassel which appears to be a part of her necklace.

The lady on the left is one of only two with a hand-maiden. Her waistline is also less shapely. This suggests that she may have been a member of the royal family. The hand-maiden on the right wears a red headband with delicate flowers painted on it. If you look closely, you will also see a pentimento, an error, just above her left breast. The frescoist originally positioned her hand in front of her breast but subsequently changed his mind. He then covered up his mistake by painting a red breast bandage referred to as thanapatiya over her breasts.

This fresco has a well-articulated face. However her body appears disproportional. Her hands are large and her fingers unusually elongated. Her ear is displaced. Her shoulder is unnatural. It may be that the face was painted by a master artist and her body by one with lesser experience.

Above: The lady on the left wears a very elaborate headdress, has an attendant and isn't as attractive as some of the others. This suggests that she may have been a member of the royal family. The attendant wears a blouse with an intricate spider-web design.

Left: The wrinkles, serious deportment, stubby fingers, and flabby forearm faithfully recreated in this painting suggest that this lady was much older than the rest. She does not wear an elaborate headdress. She may have even been the harem keeper.

Reached via a spiral metal staircase about a hundred meters above ground, the nineteen frescoes still visible today are a mere fraction of those that once adorned an immense picture gallery painted on the western rock face. The existence of a massive drip-ledge extending nearly the full extent of the western rock face and the presence of traces of plaster in an area of over five thousand six hundred square meters extending from the top of the zigzag stairway, at the south, to the northeastern to the Lion Staircase supports the view that the whole western rock face was covered in gleaming white plaster and painted with images. Several graffiti scribbled on the Mirror Wall (verses 44, 249, and 560) refer to the existence of over five hundred female figures.

Twenty-two frescoes were identified when they were first re-discovered in the late 1800s. Only nineteen survive today, protected from the elements in two adjacent depressions, referred to as Fresco Pockets A and B. Of these nineteen frescoes, two are in a very poor state of preservation.

These images offer a rare glimpse of ancient Sinhala art at its zenith. The bold representation of lithe bodies, full breasts, sensual lips, and engorged nipples are unusually erotic and provocative. They are the only open depiction of female sensuality found in Sri Lankan art. (Numerous female figures of a religious nature exist, but they follow a strictly stylized form). These paintings have been heavily influenced by the Gupta style of painting in India at this time. Given the close interaction between Buddhists of both countries, the Sigiriya artists appear to have been influenced by the *Chitrasutra* (a chapter on art contained in the sixth-century Indian text the *Visnudharmottara Purana*) and by the paintings and sculptures found in the Ajanta Caves in India. The Sigiriya frescoes, however, are judged to be far more vibrant, fluid, and lifelike than those in India. They are uniquely Sri Lankan in their character and are the only surviving secular art from antiquity found in Sri Lanka today.

In the art world, "fresco" refers to painting on fresh wet plaster with water-based paint. The painting technique used on the Sigiriya paintings is called "fresco lustro." It varies slightly from the pure fresco technique in that it also contains a mild binding agent or glue. This gives the painting added durability, as clearly demonstrated by the fact that they have survived, exposed to the elements, for over one thousand five years.

The Spiral Staircase built in 1934 leads up to the fresco pockets. Faint traces of frescoes cling precariously to the rock outside the protective enclosure.

The frescoes were painted on a plaster surface consisting of two or three distinct layers. The first layer was clay plaster. The second, when present, was a clay-lime plaster. The topmost layer was a very fine lime plaster which, when first applied, had the consistency of toothpaste.

Only red, yellow, green, and black pigments were used in the Sigiriya paintings. The red, yellow, and green colors were extracted from earth-minerals. The black pigment was charcoal black. These pigments were very robust and were impervious to the alkalinity of fresh lime plaster, and were very resistant to fading. (See Appendix B for a detailed description of how the frescoes were painted).

The chief artist was a perfectionist and a master of his craft. Not only did he strive for beauty, but he also faithfully reproduced reality in the form of wrinkles, stubby hands, thickening waistlines, and fat bulges. Given the amazingly lifelike nature of the figures in these murals, it is likely that the artist started with a reduced-scale drawing of his subject. His model, dressed in her finest, would have posed patiently for him as he drew her likeness on a rectangular painting board. Imagine the girlish excitement, the giggling and laughter, as the model conscientiously tried to maintain her composure while her friends teased her and pulled faces in an attempt the distract her. Imagine the artist, world-weary, and annoyed by their impertinence. Aware of his special place in the king's esteem, he would have trod warily, cajoling his subject to stand still, reprimanding the cheerful distractors and shooing them away. Having been given privileged access to the king's harem, he would have been especially careful never to overstep his license, for fear of the king's displeasure.

The artists worked all day, buffeted by wind, scorched by the

sun, and drenched by the rain. High above the surrounding plain, they painstakingly painted fresco after fresco in vivid and vibrant colors across the face of the rock.

The names of the ladies and the artists who painted them are lost to history. But their legacy has survived for over half a million days, smiling enigmatically, as they had done for over fifteen hundred years, a testament to the genius of their creators and the king who commissioned them.

> The masters praise delineation and articulation of form.
> The connoisseurs praise the display of light and shade.
> Women like the display of ornaments.
> The richness of colors appeals to common folks.
> The artists, therefore, should ensure that the painting is appreciated by everyone.
>
> *Visnudharmottara Purana - Chitrasutra Chapter 13*

Red clouds at sunset such as these may have been the inspiration for similar red clouds painted in the frescoes

THE FRESCO KNOWN AS B10

With a nondescript archaeological reference of B10, the fresco opposite is one of the most exquisite representations of the female form found in Sri Lankan art. Even vandals could not deface her.

Drifting atop a red sunset cloud, a beautifully ethereal smile plays upon her lips as she looks down from her celestial abode. Her left hand is in the gesture of teaching. In her upraised right hand, she holds a floral bouquet to be showered on mortals below. She appears naked from the waist up but is actually clothed in a fine gossamer blouse and is adorned with bracelets, armlets, a three-stringed pearl necklace, and another necklace with a large jeweled pendant hanging from it. She wears large earrings. Some of her red hair is gathered up in a jeweled tiara, while the rest, with flowers intertwined, flows gracefully down her back. Her eyes are light. In fact, there are numerous references in the Sigiriya Graffiti to blue water lily-colored eyes. She, too, wears the tell-tale talisman, the delicate tattoo of a woman of the king's household—a concubine. Her light eyes and red hair suggest that she was from a land far away, possibly Afghanistan.

But she isn't perfect. Painted by mere mortals, she is subject to their fallibility. If you look closely at her left hand, you will see that she has six fingers, an extra middle finger. The artist has attempted to hide his error by painting it darker than the rest, creating a shadow. It should be remembered that these paintings were intended to be viewed from afar; such minor imperfections would not have been visible.

> Priyal, having come here, saw the mountain side the long-eyed women who are separated from their lover, who is grieving for the suffering of the king, and who possess eyes like full-blown blue lilies.
>
> (Sigiriya Graffiti Verse 124)

The Frescoes Vandalized

There is unsubstantiated speculation that once Sigiriya was handed over to the Buddhist monasteries, a number of the frescoes were seen to be too sensual for a religious establishment and were removed.

The most outrageous act of vandalism, however, was committed on the night of the 13th of October 1967. On that night, vandals snuck into the unguarded Sigiriya site and made their way up to the frescoes. There they hacked away major parts of two of the frescoes leaving only small fragments of plaster

Opposite: The photograph on the left shows the restored frescoes as seen today.

Above:The same frescoes copied by DAL Perera, in 1898, show them in their original form. The lady on the right holds an a jewel-encrusted box. The yellow flowers, in free-fall, meticulously reproduced by Perera in his painting are no longer visible. They may have been lost during the restoration process.

scattered on the floor, too small for use in restoration. They also daubed green paint on fifteen of these priceless works of art. Two frescoes were lost forever. Some say it was the work of local stall-holders angry at a plan to relocate them away from the historic site. Others suggest that it was the work of zealots with a misplaced sense of puritanism. The culprits were never apprehended. Many months of painstaking restoration work was carried out to salvage these treasures. The restoration process did, however, strip some of the vibrancy from the original colors.

Etched on the surface of the Mirror Wall are nearly one thousand eight hundred pieces of prose, poetry, and commentary composed by ancient tourists. These early scribblers have left us priceless insights into the past. Of the six hundred and eighty-five individuals identified so far, twelve were women (see verse 2 below), over half identified themselves by name, many noted their social rank, and some even mentioned where they came from—towns like Weligama and Ritigala. The majority of these visitors appear to have been from the elite of society: royalty, officials, professions, and clergy. There were also soldiers, archers, and even some metalworkers. They all left their indelible musings on the Mirror Wall.

There are no graffiti scribbled on this wall prior to the sixth century. This suggests that visitors did not have access to the site for about two hundred years after Sigiriya was abandoned as a royal citadel. As the monastery started to fall into hard times, it may have supplemented its income by allowing visitors and pilgrims to see the rather titillating frescoes. This interpretation is supported by the fact that several clay figurines have been found on site, which appear to be souvenirs of the frescoes. The last graffiti was scribbled in the fourteenth century. This coincided with the collapse of the Polonnaruwa Kingdom and the abandonment of Sigiriya as a monastic compound.

Most of the graffiti are written in Sinhala and Sanskrit. A few are written in Tamil. They are secular in nature. While some may be considered slightly titillating, none appear to be overtly lewd. In fact, a very high level of deference was shown to the ladies of the frescoes. Where some have erred, others have scratched out the offending comments. The topics range from love to satire, curses, wit, and lament. Many demonstrate a very high level of literacy and a deep appreciation of art and poetry.

Curiously, none refer to King Kasyapa as a parricide. None refer to the frescoes as having any religious context. None refer to the original site as anything other than a royal palace. Nearly forty inscribers refer to the king and the ladies of the royal household, reaffirming the view that Sigiriya was a royal residence of Kasyapa and that these were ladies of Kasyapa's harem.

Wet with cool dew drops
fragrant with perfume from the flowers
came the gentle breeze
jasmine and water lily
dance in the spring sunshine
side-long glances
of the golden-hued ladies
stab into my thoughts
heaven itself cannot take my mind
as it has been captivated by one lass
among the five hundred I have seen here.

A deer-eyed maiden of the mountain side arouses
anger in my mind.
In her hand, she holds a string of pearls,
and in her eyes, she assumes rivalry with me.

We spoke, but they did not answer
Those ladies of the mountain
They did not give us
The twitch of an eyelid.

The girl with the golden skin enticed the mind and eyes.
Ladies like you make men pour out their hearts
And you also have thrilled the body
Making it stiffen with desire.

The five hundred damsels arrest the progress of
him who is going to heaven.
With their gentle smile and the fluttering of their
eye-lids, the damsels stood here, enslaved me who
had come to the summit of the cliff.

The golden-colored ones on the mountain-side
have the appearance of those hurling themselves
down from the summit of the rock, their hearts
not being able to bear up because of grief, since
the king indeed is dead.

In what manner did they,
having ascended the mountainside,
look at this one and make her remain here,
making her not speak,
just as it was done in those days of King Kasubu.

Do not look at that.
Let us go away rejecting, the golden colored one
whose breasts are drooped.
They reside on a ruined wall on the summit of the rock.
They speak not even though we speak.

Lion Staircase

Situated on a small escarpment known as the Plateau of Red Arsenic, the paws and staircase are all that remain of a once colossal gatehouse built in the form of a sphinx-like lion which guarded the final entrance to the inmost sanctum of the entire complex: the palace of the god-king on the summit. Gazing northwards, over a vista that stretches to the horizon, it was thirty-five meters high, twenty-one meters wide, and protruded eleven meters from the rock face. Brightly colored, eyes ablaze, and its mouth agape it, appeared ready to swallow anyone who dared approach it. It is the only feature specifically mentioned in the *Culavamsa*; Sīhāgiri – the Lion Rock.

Seated on a specially built plinth, this recumbent lion was made of heavily plastered masonry and wood. The grooves and holes chiseled into the rock provide us with clues to the size and position of the lion's head. Especially molded bricks shaped to accentuate the contour of the structure were used. These can still be seen on the paws and toes of the lion. Traces of the original plaster, over two inches thick, are also still visible on the paw today. Traces of plaster on the rock face above this colossus suggest that it too was painted with frescoes.

Given Kasyapa's fondness for flamboyancy, to further shock and awe visitors, some have suggested that, it was designed to gush forth a spectacular torrent of water from its mouth. One may even imagine that the water was dyed red for further effect. This water was supplied from a pond on the north via a channel cut into the rock. On special occasions, large lamps were lit at night behind the lion's eyes to further impress all around.

A semi-circular granite moonstone lies at the base of a narrow flight of limestone steps leading up to an entryway that was once protected by cleverly disguised doors that opened out from the mane on the lion's chest. Just inside this entryway was another flight of stairs which proceeded in zigzag fashion inside the lion's head and reappeared behind the head. The stairs then lead up a passageway to the palace on the summit. Other than the clearly visible heavily grooved rock face just above this structure, there is

Artist's impression of the Lion Staircase. It was probably more elaborately decorated.

no evidence of the passage and stairway that led to the top. This stairway probably had limestone steps and may have had a roof. It is reasonable to assume that it was of a similar style to that of the Mirror Wall.

It appears that the lion may have survived in relatively good preservation until about the ninth century, a span of four hundred years, before its timber structures finally gave way, and the entire structure crumbled. There are several graffiti on the Mirror Wall referring to the Lion. One such reads:

> Having ascended Sigiriya to see what is there
>
> I fulfilled my mind's desire
>
> and saw His Lordship the Lion.

Kasyapa's choice of a lion is an interesting twist to our story. The lion is symbolic of kingship and the basis of the foundation myth of the Sinhalese people. According to folklore, Sinhabahu—the mythical ancestor of the Sinhalese people—was said to have been born as a result of a union between a lion and a princess. He assassinated his father, the lion, to escape from his lair. His son, Vijay, the first king of Lanka, was forced to flee his homeland and serendipitously landed on the island of Lanka. One can only wonder if the symbolism was not lost on Kasyapa.

H.C.P. Bell discovered an enormous pile of rubble, which appears to have been the remains of the head of the lion, at the base of the rock when he commenced excavation of the site in the late 1890s. Unfortunately, this was cleared and disposed of by Bell during his conservation work. He also uncovered a number of courtyards, pavilions, and other structures on this small plateau. The vintage of these structures is uncertain. However, given Kasyapa's high aesthetic sensibility, it is most likely that this area contained a large open courtyard to enhance the impact of the lion staircase. A number of pavilions and courtyards at the extreme north probably served as a reception area, or maybe even a rest stop on the way to the summit. The remnants of a stone staircase exist at the extreme northern end of this plateau and disappear into a steep precipice. It has been suggested that this alternate stairway was partially built of wood and intended for easy destruction in case of an attack.

Especially molded bricks shaped to accentuate the contours of the structure were used. These can still be seen on the paws and toes of the lion. Traces of the original plaster, over two inches thick, is also visible.

This stone staircase at the northern end of the Plateau of Arsenic disappears abruptly into a steep precipice below. It has been suggested that this alternate stairway was used regularly as it made access to the summit easier and faster. Partially built of timber it was intended for easy destruction in case of an attack.

The Summit

The summit of the Sigiriya rock is in the form of an elliptical stepped plateau of about one and a half hectares, with a gradual slope along the long north-south axis of the ellipse. This sloping contour is part natural and part man-made. The palace complex on top of the summit was the innermost sanctum and the geometrical center of the Sigiriya complex. Only the king, queen, and a small retinue of staff lived there. It is the earliest and best-preserved palace complex in Sri Lanka. The sheer scale and the complexity of these structures on the summit have made it extremely difficult to ascertain the purpose of most of the ruins.

When H.C.P. Bell and his team reached the summit in 1895, they found it engulfed in an impenetrable canopy of trees and vegetation. They set about burning off the vegetation, which then revealed faint traces of the royal compound buried beneath between two to six meters of debris. The whole area was cleared, and the rubble scooped up into wicker baskets and tossed over the side. Unfortunately, these crude methods of archeological excavation may have erased many tell-tales artifacts that modern archeologists would have found useful. Bell was astounded by the extent of the ruins, which covered the entire summit and extended to the very edge of the rock. The locals also claimed that there was a passage from the summit into the bowels of the rock, but this is not the case.

The entire summit was surrounded by a stout brick wall built to the very edge of the rock, the footings of which are still clearly visible today. This wall offered protection from high winds and monsoonal rain. Painted white like the rest of the rock, it looked to a person standing below as though it was an extension of the rock itself.

Given the susceptibility to high winds, the buildings were squat, solidly built, single-story structures with low-profile roofs. Since clay roofing tiles would have blown off in windy weather, the roofs were made predominately of wood. We are not certain if these were wooden planks or tiles, as no traces of them have been found. The discovery of large quantities of iron and copper nails on the summit suggests that the roofs were firmly battened down with nails and rope. Consistent with the architecture of the time,

The massive scale of the palace complex on the summit of the rock can be gauged by the people visible in the photograph (top right).

On the highest point on the summit was a stupa and royal mansion (sleeping quarters). To the left immediately under the overhang of the rock in can be seen the paws of the Lion Staircase. Below the Lion Staircase is an area some call the Guardhouse. The true purpose of the buildings there is not known. The lighter area extending almost the full breadth of the side of the rock was once painted with frescoes. Traces of white plaster can still be seen in places clinging to the rock surface. The Fresco Pocket, the Spiral Staircase, Mirror Wall and Grand Staircases are also visible. In the foreground to the right is the Cistern Rock and Audience Hall. The two large boulders in the front foreground show traces of building footings suggesting that they once had pavilions build on top of them.

there were many pillared pavilions which allowed cooling air to waft freely through them.

It is most likely that the summit palace was predominantly used during the dry season. Given its high elevation of nearly three hundred and sixty meters above sea-level, it would have been a cool and comforting place, away from flies and mosquitoes. During the wet monsoon season, from May to September, the lower palaces were most likely used.

The complex is divided into two sections: the Royal Compound occupying the northwestern and northeastern part of the summit; and the Gardens and service quarters to the south. A walkway paved with marble slabs runs down the center of the complex. Limestone and quartz blocks were also used for paving the stairways and passages throughout the summit. Their light color and luminosity complemented the vivid white walls and were said to glow in the moonlight.

Prudent water management was used throughout. Rainwater runoff was carefully harvested and stored in large cisterns and ponds on the summit. Excess runoff was channeled into a cistern below the rock. When required, an army of water-carriers was employed to transport water up to the summit. It has been suggested that pumps and windmills were used. This is fanciful. No supporting evidence exists, and the necessary technology was unknown at the time.

A small stupa occupied the highest point of the summit next The ruins of a small stupa occupied the highest point of the summit next to the inner palace. It probably replaced a lightning-tower which once stood there. Having built some of the tallest buildings in the ancient world, Sri Lankan architects were well aware of the devastating impacts of lightning strikes. With its metal-tipped pinnacle, the lightning-tower acted as an excellent lightning rod, deflecting lightning strikes away from the royal mansion.

The royal mansion with a single room measuring thirteen by seven meters is believed to have been the kings sleeping quarters. It consists of an inner chamber surrounded by a narrow corridor and an exterior wall. This extra bulwark may have lessened the impact of wind buffeting on the summit and allowed its occupants a sound night's sleep.

This double-walled building was probably the kings sleeping quarters.

All that remains of a stupa that occupied the highest point of the summit is a small pile of rubble. This was a later addition. Prior to that there may have been a lightning-tower With its metal-tipped pinnacle deflecting lightning strikes away from the royal mansion.

Located above the large pond this stone throne was carved out of the surrounding rock. Facing east and aligning with the central east-west axis of the complex; it provides an uncluttered vista to the horizon. The post holes on the floor indicate that a four-posted canopy was erected to provide shade and protection. A grooved channel carved behind the seat prevented water from draining down into it.

In these Royal Gardens on the summit grew plants with colorful fruits and flowers. There are traces of successive reconstructions of the garden beds, but the earliest of these is clearly from Kasyapa's time.

The purpose of these hallows is not fully understood. They may have been lookouts or just quaint vantage points from which to reflect on the lake and the vista below.

Above & Next Page: The Large Pond measures twenty-seven by twenty-one meters. All sections of the compound converged on this pond. It was obviously central to the summit complex. The western side of the pond was hewn from the rock, and the other three sides were built up with stone slabs and bricks. The walls were plastered and colorfully decorated. Several stairways lead to, from, and within this pond area.

The Sigiriya citadel can be seen in the center of this photograph. To the north is Pidurangala. To the south is the Sigiriya Mahavava and just below it, further to the south, is the Mapagala Complex. The extension of the rampart across the lake is also clearly visible.

GREATER SIGIRIYA AREA

Sigiriya was not restricted merely to the fortified refuge of a monarch. It was, in fact, a well-planned and vibrant city several square kilometers in extent. Most of the city structures being made of brick and timber have long since vanished. The remnants of numerous reservoirs and channels are the clearest evidence that the area was once extensively cultivated and populated.

Sigiri Mahavava located to the southeast was once a massive man-made lake which supplied water to the citadel and large parts of the surrounding city. Its earthen dam extended for a distance of over eight kilometers. This tank was bisected by the outer ramparts of the citadel providing a secure internal water supply to the fortress.

The Mapagala Complex, to the south of the citadel, was built prior to the construction of the Sigiri Mahavava. This has led to speculation that the site was occupied before the fifth century AD. Its outer wall is constructed of massive blocks of gneissic-granite. It is the first example of large scale construction around the Sigiriya area.

Pidurangala located north of the citadel also dominates the surrounding landscape with its unusual triangular rock silhouette. The monastery there was first established around the third century BC. Inscriptions dating to the 5th and 7th centuries confirm that this is, in fact, the Dalaha Vihara referred to in the *Culavamsa*. Given these inscriptions and the fact that the road from the north gate of the citadel leads directly to the temple suggests that this was the temple at which Kasyapa worshiped. On the top of the hill, reached by a rough flight of steps is a large cave 60 meters in length. Inside is a statue of a reclining Buddha. The statue is very similar in style to a reclining Buddha statue in the Ajanta Caves in India. It is possible that the ancient artisans gained inspiration while visiting Ajanta but applied a uniquely Sri Lankan twist to their work. Remnants of paint on the pillow and soles of feet indicated that the entire statue was once painted.

SCULPTURES AT ANURADHAPURA

There are no notable sculptures or statues at Sigiriya. However, there are two found at Isurumuniya temple at Anuradhapura that have been dated to about the time of Kasyapa's reign. Given that Kasyapa renovated this temple extensively, the sculptures are secular in nature and follow the Gupta style, suggests that these were commissioned by Kasyapa.

5th-century carving believed to be that of a royal family. May even be that of Kasyapa and his family as we know he had two daughters as depicted.

Next page: The Isurumuniya Lovers. 5th century Gupta style sculptor. Probably depicting Saliya and Asokamala but using the painting of "two lovers" found in the Ajanta Caves in India as his inspiration.

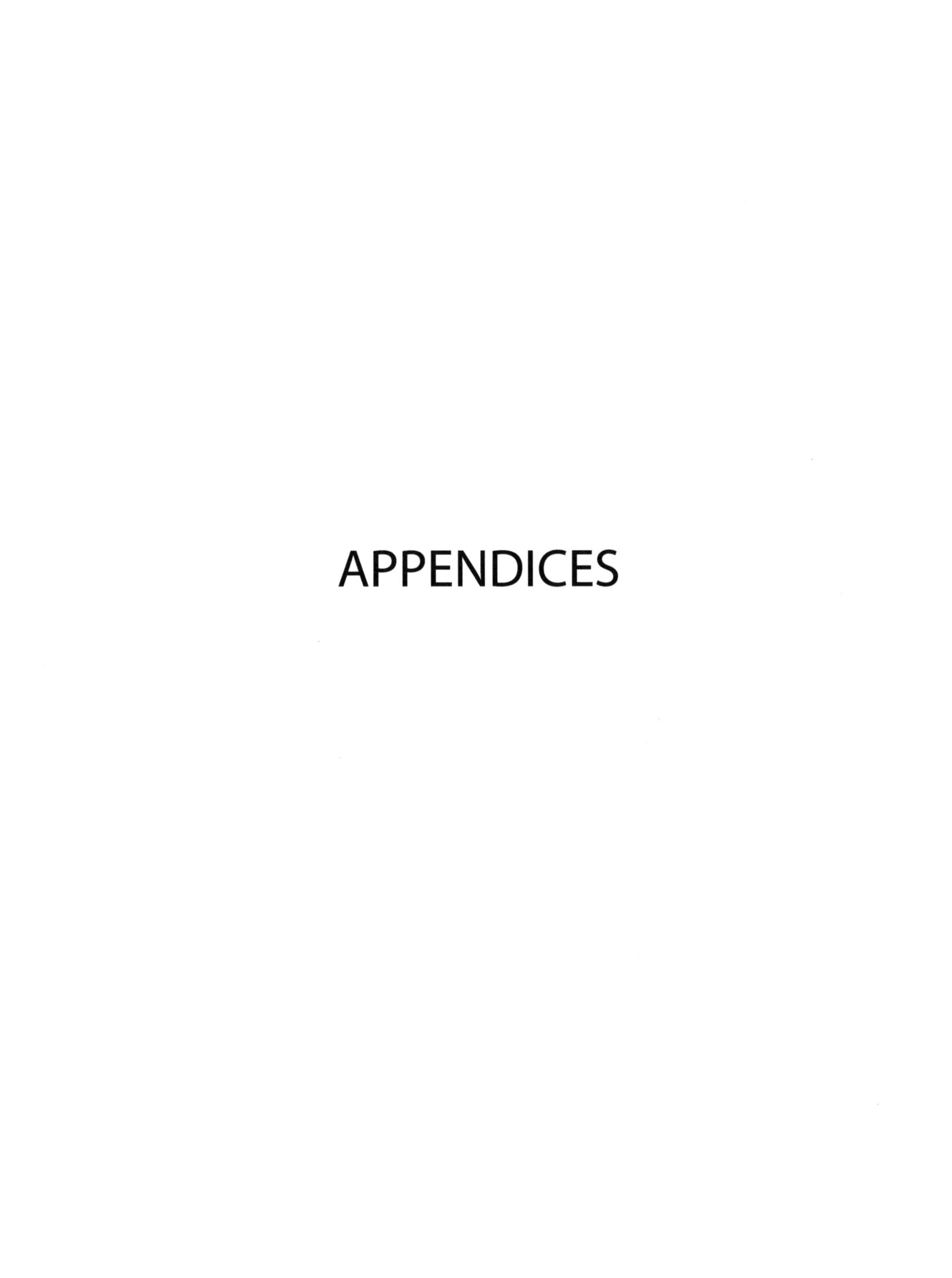

APPENDICES

Appendix A - The Harem (Orodha) - Women of the Royal Household

The ladies of the royal household, the *orodha* or *antepura*, were an integral part of the fabric of society and government. More commonly referred to as a "harem" in western society, it is often portrayed as a vile and exploitative institution. Any reference today to the institution of the harem immediately conjures up in the western mind scantily clad young women forced into slavery, solely for the sexual gratification of a powerful man. This is a grossly distorted view of the institution, especially in Sri Lanka. The Arabic term "harem" conveys the notion of taboo and generally refers to prohibition. The Pali word "orodha" meaning "behind the curtain", implies a more sequestered existence. It usually referred to all the women of the royal household. Polygamy was a deeply entrenched privilege of kingship. It was a social institution that was so much the norm that it gets scant mention in the *Mahavamsa* or any other historical document of the time.

The king had only one queen-wife who was, without exception, of royal or noble lineage. (The only exception to this rule was Subha's daughter Mahamatta). It was only a male offspring of a queen-wife who had the right of kingship. In our story, this was rightly Moggallana. No other offspring was entitled to any special entitlement other than that which may be bestowed on them by the king. In addition to the single officially designated queen-wife, kings maintained a number of lesser wives and concubines. Being an expensive extravagance to upkeep, the number of women in the king's household was seen as a measure of his wealth, power, and influence.

The orodha played an important role in society. Young princesses and girls of noble birth joined the orodha to cement relationships between the king and foreign and local rulers. It also offered an opportunity for attractive and talented women of lowly birth to better themselves and their families. It trained them in the social and cultural graces.

Being a member of the king's harem was a badge of honor, bringing prestige to her and to her family. In the context of the times, the orodha wasn't necessarily oppressive or demeaning of women. Other than royal relatives, membership in the orodha was temporary. The pool of women in the royal harem was continuously refreshed. New entrants were chosen for their youth, beauty, or social connections. Women from all walks of life could be selected for service in the harem. These ranged from princesses from foreign countries, daughters of chieftains and high-class families, girls from lower socioeconomic standing sold by their families in the hope of improving their lot, "slave girls" gifted from foreign rulers and others selected for their beauty. There is no evidence of direct cohesion or kidnapping. These women having more face-time with the king than all but his closest advisors could bring significant benefits to herself and her family. A woman could eventually depart the royal harem wealthy, well connected and in high demand; her beauty, etiquette , and knowledge of the court enabling her to marry or work in elite households.

Wives, sisters, mothers, consorts, concubines and young children lived together in a familial environment in secluded quarters in a large compound. The entire staff of this compound was women. At Sigiriya, this compound was probably the central ramparted area in the still to be excavated eastern precinct.

The nominal head of the harem was the Queen-Mother. Day to day management was in the hands of the harem keeper, usually an older woman, who ensured order was maintained and the king satisfied.

The lives of the women in the harem were mostly those of pampered boredom. It was a far more congenial existence than they might otherwise have experienced outside. They spent their lives keeping up with the latest fashions, trying to make themselves as alluring as possible to catch the eye of a king and to maintain their position in the hierarchy of the harem. Their other duties included child rearing and wet nursing. At Sigiriya, these ladies probably spent many hours in the lavish western precinct with its pavilions, gardens, and pools.

Occasional public outings were always in the company of the King. These were a lavish affair with the ladies dressed in beautiful clothing and spectacular adornments intended to impress.

There is no direct evidence of women of the harem being tattooed. This lack of evidence doesn't preclude the fact that it may have been the case. This practice is known to have occurred elsewhere. Given the prestige attached to being a member of the orodha, there is little reason to doubt that these ladies would have gladly worn their delicately etched tattoos with pride.

Tattooed females only appear in the Sigiriya frescoes.

Appendix B - How The Frescoes Were Painted

The Sigiriya paintings are called frescoes. In the art world, "fresco" refers to painting on fresh or wet plaster. The term has been corrupted somewhat and is sometimes used more generically to mean a wall mural. The painting technique used on the Sigiriya paintings is called "fresco lustro." It is an ancient painting technique used in India and Sri Lanka and was not well known in the West.

In the bueno fresco method, pigment suspended in water is applied directly onto wet plaster. It contains no binding agents such as gum or glue. As the plaster dries, the calcium hydroxide from the plaster seeps toward the surface and through the paint layer, where it reacts with the air to form a protective deposit of calcium carbonate, locking in the paint underneath this lime skin as though it was sealed in glass. This gives it outstanding durability. This was the technique used by Michelangelo in the Sistine Chapel a thousand years after the frescoes at Sigiriya.

In the secco (secco means "dry" in Italian) technique, pigment is mixed with a binding agent containing glue or gum and applied on dry plaster. The glue fixes the pigment to the surface as it dries. These paintings are easier to do but have a tendency to peel and flake off. Most murals, including those in the Ajanta Caves, use this technique.

In the fresco lustro technique (sometimes referred to as the Rajasthani or Ala-gali), the painting is executed on wet plaster as with the buon fresco technique, but a binding agent is also mixed with the pigment, as in the secco technique. Possessing the benefits of both the buon and secco methods, paintings executed in fresco lustro have exceptionally high levels of adhesion and are extremely durable and resistant to weathering, as demonstrated in the Sigiriya painting.

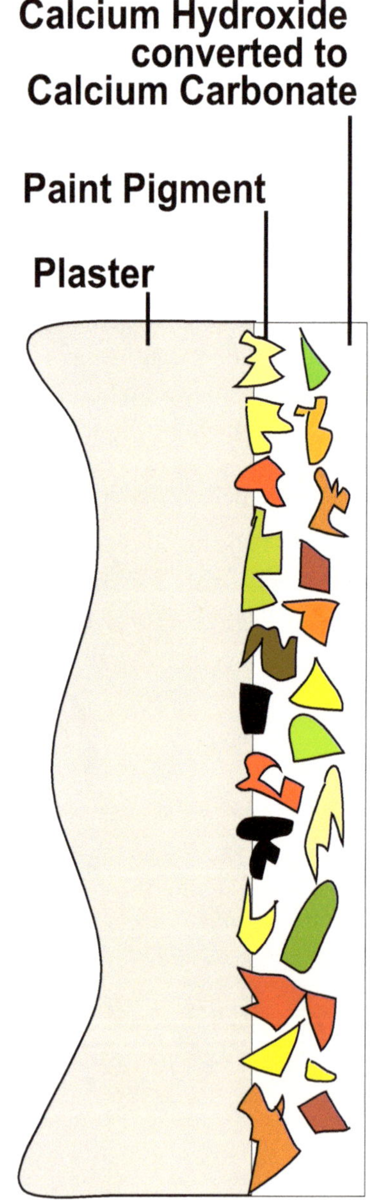

The diagram shows how pigments are fixed into the calcium carbonate layer in bueno fresco paintings

The Sigiriya frescoes were painted on a plaster surface, which consisted of three, but sometimes only two, distinct layers. The first layer was clay plaster. The second, when present, was a clay-lime plaster. The final, topmost, layer was a very fine lime plaster.

According to the *Manjusribhasita-Vastuvidyasastra* (also known as the *Chitrakarmasastra* that was probably based on the older Indian

Visnudharmottara Purana), an ancient Sri Lankan manual on monastic architecture, clay plaster was manufactured from clay collected near a well or reservoir. It was sifted to remove impurities and dried on a slate surface. Ingredients such as gold, silver, copper, sugar, honey, pepper, dry ginger, cardamom, yellow orpiment (arsenic sulfide), parts of the chebulic myrobalan tree, sal tree resin (Shorea robusta), and sulfur were added. Then shape coarse sand was added in the ratio one part sand to four parts clay. Coconut water was used to moisten the mixture, which was then kneaded until consistent. This mixture was then allowed to cure in a copper vessel for at least one month.

We don't have a recipe for the manufacture of the clay-lime plaster of the second layer.

The preparation of the limestone plaster of the final topmost layer is also given in the *Chitrakarmasastra*. Lime was generally obtained from large outcrops of pure lime, which the *Chitrakarmasastra* claims could be found close to large water sources. This was sometimes supplemented with lime extracted from coral or seashells. The raw material was powdered and roasted over a wood fire until the carbon dioxide was driven out of it. This was mixed with water, the juice extracted from the pulp of the wood apple fruit, and the extract of three types of myrobalan trees and slaked for a number of years in underground storage pits until it had the consistency of a buttery slurry. It was then strained through a fine sieve to remove all coarse particles. This paste was then mixed with the resin extracted from the bark of the wood apple tree, cotton wool, milk curd, egg white, fenugreek (*Trigonella foenum-graecum*), and jaggery (an unrefined sugar). These organic compounds were added to the plaster to give it spreadability, durability, and luster. The end product was similar in consistency to modern-day toothpaste: soft, silky smooth, and homogeneous.

Wood Apple (Limonia acidissima, divul in Sinhala)

Stone Apple (Aegle marmelos, beli in Sinhalese)

Recent scientific analysis of the clay plaster layer found it to contain clay rich in iron, sand, and black stone grit. It also contained paddy husk, straw, and coconut fibers. These organic fibers were mixed into the clay before application to add tensile strength to the plaster and to prevent it from cracking. The second layer revealed that it consists predominantly of lime, sand, and black stone grit, but it also contained traces of sugar and amino acids, suggesting the presence of gum and proteins. These organic compounds may have been the result of the addition of binding agents such as the pulp from the fruit of the stone apple tree milk curd, and jaggery. The topmost layer on analysis was found to contain lime, fine sand, and traces of sugar, carbohydrates, and proteins. High concentrations of carbohydrate molecules, similar to those found in the wood apple tree, were identified. The presence of proteins is consistent with the use of substances such as milk curd and egg whites. The presence of sugar is consistent with the use of raw sugar.

Only red, yellow, green, and black pigments were used in the Sigiriya paints. These colors were most suitable, as they were earth-mineral based and did not deteriorate as a result of the alkalinity of fresh lime plaster. Red was from red ochre, obtained by pulverizing natural earth containing about 95 percent ferric oxide. The yellow color was derived from yellow ochre from the mineral goethite (iron oxyhydroxide). Another ancient Indian document, called the *Silparatna*, describes how to extract this pigment. The rock containing goethite was collected and ground into a fine powder. This was mixed with water and the solution allowed to settle. The substance that floated on the top was collected and the whole process repeated until the substance floated in clear water. It was then smeared on a new earthen pot and allowed to dry in the sun. The dried yellow pigment was then collected for use. The green pigment was obtained from the minerals celadonite and glauconite. It was ground into a fine powder and placed in a container of water for two to three days. The color permeated into the water. This colored water as then used. The black pigment was lampblack obtained by burning a lamp and collecting soot in an inverted pot. All the color pigments were suspended in water containing wood apple gum, which the tree exudes from trunk and branches during wet weather. As mentioned earlier, only mineral-based colors were used, as the lime would "burn" organic and vegetable colors. The color blue is not present in the paintings, as the types of blue available at the time were azurite blue and lapis lazuli, both of which were not suitable with wet lime plaster.

Scientific analysis of the paint used on the frescoes confirmed the existence of all of the compounds referred to above. Carbohydrate polymers similar to those of the resin of the wood apple tree were clearly detected. There was also no evidence that vegetable pigments were used in the paintings.

We do not have direct evidence of the brushes used for these paintings. However, the *Chitrakarmasastra* prescribes that brushes could have been made from hair collected from the ear of a calf, the belly of a goat, the tail of a muskrat, or the tail of a squirrel, the whiskers of a cat or rat, the tips of grasses, et cetera.

Work on the frescoes would have started probably in about the second year of the construction project. Tens of thousands of pieces of bamboo were transported to the site in carts. These were then assembled into a massive latticework of scaffolding extending from the base of the rock all the way to the summit two hundred meters above. The latticework was anchored to the top of the rock and at points along the side to provide a reasonable degree of rigidity to the structure. The whole erection was held together with nothing more than coir rope made from coconut fiber. There were no ladders or safety rails. Access to the working platforms was by clambering up the scaffolding's bamboo cross members. The bamboo scaffolding offered no heavy load-bearing areas. Therefore, pulley systems or other mechanized methods were not employed. All raw materials were hauled up by hand.

Stonemasons were the first to commence work on the rock face. Having been briefed by the chief artist on the proposed position of the gallery, they determined the most suitable place to chisel out a drip ledge. The purpose of a drip ledge was to prevent water from flowing down the natural curvature of

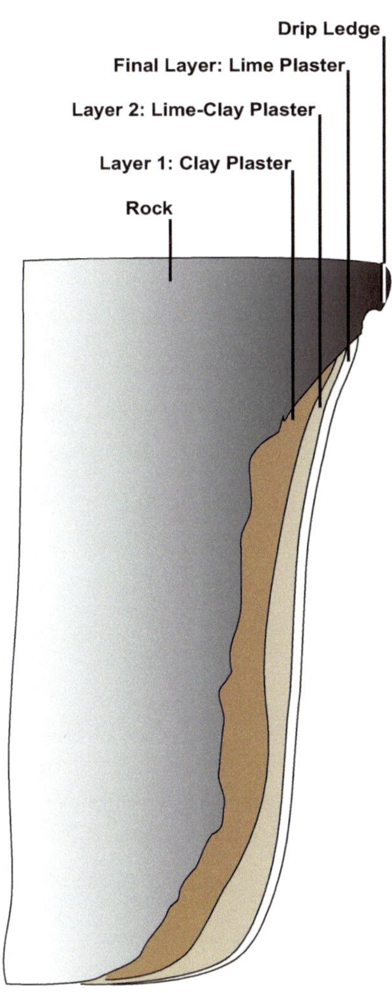

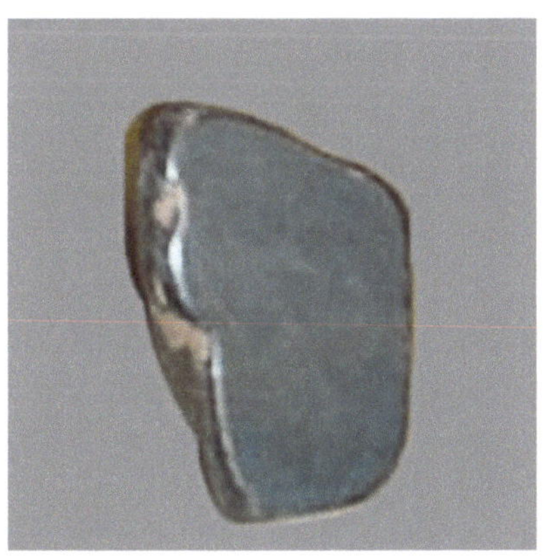

Agate similar to that used to smoothen plaster

the rock. The drip ledge created a slight lip from which the water dropped off the rock instead. Using stone pounders and iron chisels, the masons set to work carving out the drip ledge and then roughening and scouring the surface of the rock below it where the frescoes were to be painted. The roughened surface was required to provide a good grip for the plaster grounding.

The plasterers followed the stonemasons. They cleaned the surface thoroughly, removing any residual debris and dust. The first layer of clay plaster was intended to provide solid bonding with the underlying rock surface and smooth out any major surface imperfections. It was applied in two coatings to build up the necessary thickness. The first coating of plaster was thrown sharply at the rock from a distance of about sixty centimeters so that it splattered and stuck to the surface, minimizing air bubbles. It was flattened in an upward direction to remove any remaining air bubbles and get better adhesion. It was then beaten firmly into the rock surface and allowed to partially dry out. The beating of the plaster was very important and was carried out throughout the plastering process. When beaten, the grains of sharp sand in the mixture compressed and interlocked with each other, giving a much stronger bond. The second coating was applied an the identical manner as the first. It, too, was beaten firmly and molded into the desired shape. It was burnished with a smooth agate stone and allowed to partially dry out.

The second layer was about half an inch thick. It consisted of clay-lime plaster and was applied over the first layer before it had completely dried and cured. The first layer was wetted down with clean water and rubbed with a wad made of coconut fibers until it loosened sufficiently a form a skim coat. This was to ensure that the second layer bonded well with the first. Once the second layer had been applied, it too was beaten to remove excess moisture and encourage good adhesion. It was then molded as required, smoothened out and then the surface was roughened slightly with a comb in preparation of the final coat.

The final layer was also applied before the layer below

it completely dried. It consisted of slurry applied with a trowel. Once this layer was sufficiently congealed it too was gently beaten and then while still wet carefully burnished and polished over and over again with agate stones leaving a smooth off-white surface for the artist to work on.

The plasterers and artists worked closely together. The plasterers prepared the surfaces, and the artists then painted on the final layer while it was still wet. Because these are fresco paintings and had to be drawn on wet plaster, the topmost surface was laid down in new sections each day. At the start of each day, the edges of the previous day's top-most layer was scrapped away to the clay-lime layer with a rod-like tool and a new section of lime plaster laid abutting the previous section. This new section was usually left for a day or so to harden.

The chief artist was a master of his craft. With years of experience, he was well versed in the *Chitrasutra*. He had probably visited the Ajanta Caves in India and marveled at the paintings and sculptures there.

Given the amazing lifelike nature of the figures in these murals, it is likely that the artist started with a reduced scale drawing of his subject drawn on a rectangular painting board. These drawings were probably done during the wet session, at the court at Anuradhapura, when much work could not be carried out on the frescoes.

Each morning the chief artist, painting boards in hand, would have the laborious climb up the scaffolding to the location of the day's painting. Once there, he personally examined the plaster by pressing his finger into it to ensure that it was ripe for painting. In fresco painting, the artist must always be keenly aware of the ever-changing nature of the medium as it undergoes a number of transformations while it dries. He, in turn, must adjust his technique to suit the thirstiness of the plaster.

Using a fine brush dipped in red paint, he deftly sketched the outline of his compositions in graceful, steady, smooth, and free-flowing lines. He would have reminded himself that beauty lay in the simplicity of form and the least number of lines. Never a crooked line, never an uneven line was his mantra as he quickly added sufficient detail to the drawing to be confident that his team of less-skilled artists would be able to fill in color and detail. The chief artist was a perfectionist. Not only did he strive for beauty, but he also faithfully reproduced wrinkles, stubby hands, thickening waistlines, fat bulges, fingernails, and lots more.

In the first four hours, plaster was soggy and averse to absorbing paint. Paint had to be applied loosely with a small, semi-dry brush, the pigment beaten into the surface without breaking the skin. Too much paint would have dripped off, ruining the day's work. As the day progressed and the plaster dried, its absorption characteristics improved. During this phase, long, sweeping brushstrokes of light colors were applied. Stroke atop stroke of thin, watery paint was applied until the desired intensity of color and depth was achieved. As the plaster was saturated with paint, it acquired a beautiful, marble-like sheen. They knew that too much paint at this stage would cause irreparable drips and thick blotches of color. Too little paint, on the other hand, would cause the plaster to suck the paint too quickly, leaving whitish dry spots. It was a delicate balance. As the plaster continued to dry, it became

more ravenous for water and absorbed color greedily. At this stage, it was best to paint the outlines and areas that required the darkest shades of color. It was at this time that the final and most important aspect of the painting was undertaken. Known as the "opening of the eyes," great significance was attached to this aspect of painting. Improperly done, the hapless subject could be cursed with bad luck for the rest of her life. Only the chief artist would have been entrusted with this delicate ritual. It was he who breathed life into the painting by performing the final and most important detail to be painted.

They had worked all day, buffeted by wind, scorched by the sun, and drenched by the rain. High above the surrounding plain they worked, painstakingly painted fresco after fresco in vivid and vibrant colors across the face of the rock. Only nineteen frescoes survive today, protected from the elements in two adjacent depressions referred to as Fresco Pocket A and B. There is unsubstantiated speculation that once Sigiriya was handed over to the Buddhist monasteries, a number of the frescoes were removed, as they were seen to be too sensual for a religious establishment. On October 13, 1967, vandals hacked away major parts of two of the frescoes and daubed green paint on these and twelve other frescoes. Fortunately, all but two of the frescoes were painstaking restored.

Coir rope made of coconut fiber used to tie bamboo scaffolding

Appendix C - Alternate Histories

A number of alternate interpretations of Sigiriya have recently been put forward. It is the author's view that they have not been subjected to rigorous analysis and debate to debunk the story in the *Culavamsa.* These theories are summarized below.

A Palace of a Mountain King ('Parvataraja')

The eminent archaeologist and historian Senarat Paranavitana, in his book titled *The Story of Sigiriya*, claimed to have deciphered an alternate history of Kasyapa inscribed on stone slabs by a monk named Ananda in the 15th Century AD. In this version of history,Kasyapa was not a patricide, and Sigiriya was merely a manifestation of his desire to attain the status of a god-king (Kuvera). While the basic premise of this story, namely that Kasyapa desired to attain the position of a god-king is plausible and corroborated by the *Culavamsa.* The subsequent detailed account of events, however, is fanciful. It is indeed a very long and detailed story to be carved as a stone inscription in the 15th century. The inscriptions hold no religious tract and bear no royal proclamation. One can only ask why the inscriber expended so much effort in telling a rather inconsequential story a thousand years after Kasyapa's death. In other words, these so-called inscriptions hold no merit to justify their existence. To date, these interlinear inscriptions and Paranavitana's interpretation of them have not been validated by any other epigraphist or archaeologist. A good rebuttal to this theory is provided by Ananda Guruge in *Senarat Paranavitana as a Writer of Historic Fiction in Sanskrit.*

A Buddhist Monastery

Raja de Silva, a former Commissioner of Archaeology, in his book *Sigiriya and its Significance,* has put forward a different hypothesis to explain Sigiriya's existence. According to de Silva, Sigiriya was actually a Mahayana Buddhist monastery. This monastic complex was built over hundreds of years and ceased to exist around the 12th century. De Silva argues that the frescoes are not of Kasyapa's consorts, cloud damsels, lightning princesses or apsaras, but rather that they depict the goddess Tara Devi (mother goddess). This hypothesis too, suffers from numerous shortcomings. Why is a religious establishment surrounded by a formidable array of moats and ramparts? How did a monastic establishment have the financial wherewithal to maintain such an extravagant establishment such as Sigiriya so far away from any urban centers which could have offered it sustenance? Why is the goddess Tara depicted in so many different manifestations and sometimes rather unflattering in appearance? Why are there no significant Stupas, inscriptions or carving in a formidable religious establishment which is said to have spanned over a thousand years? Why are there no references to this monastic establishment any verifiable inscription? Why do none of the over 1300 graffiti refer to a monastery or make any reference to the ladies in the frescoes as the Goddess Tara? While de Silva makes a very forceful argument his theory has not been accepted by the wider archeological community.

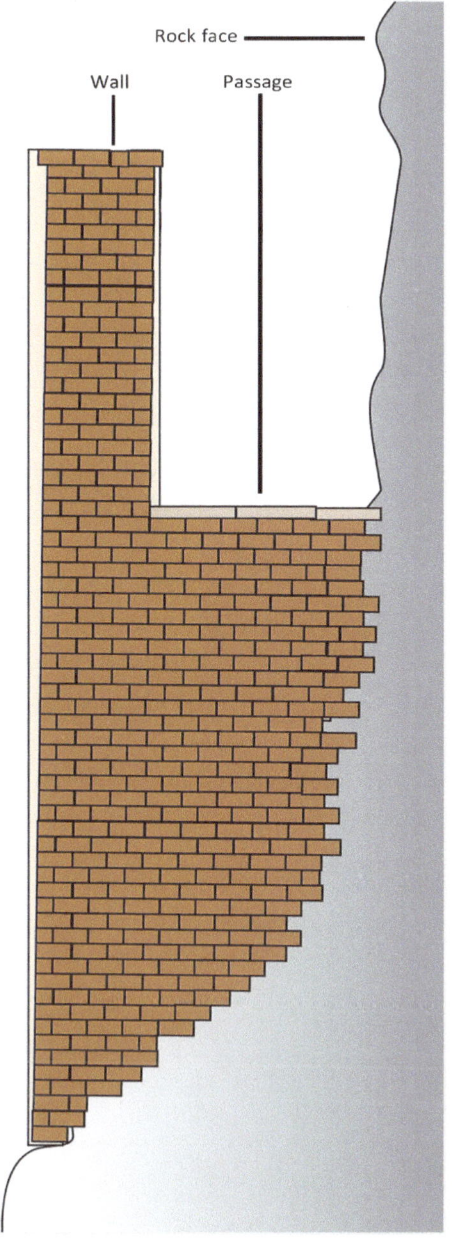

Appendix D- How The Mirror Wall Was Built

Faced with a near-vertical rock face, the ancient builders exploited any natural indentation in the side of the rock to provide support for their wall. They did this by dropping a plumb bob (plumb line) from the proposed location of the outside of the wall until they hit a protruding rock surface far below. At this spot, a flat niche wide enough to support at least a single brick was carved out along the entire length of the wall. Then a series of parallel grooves, each at least a brick-width deep, were cut up the side of the rock to the point where the floor of the passageway was to be constructed.

Then a solid parapet wall of varying thickness (depending on the contour of the rock face) was built up to the height of the passageway, while some of the outer bricks were built up further to form the exterior wall. The bricks were laid slightly off horizontal—that is to say, with a slight inclination toward the rock. This slight inclination pushes the overall weight of the structure toward the wall, giving it better adherence to the rock face. The brickwork of the wall, too, is slightly off perpendicular, leaning inward.

BIBLIOGRAPHY

References

Agrawal, Om Prakash, & Nanda Amara Wickramasinghe. Materials & Techniques of Ancient Wall Paintings of Sri Lanka. New Delhi: Sundeep Prakashan, 2002. Print.

Bandaranayake, Senake. "The 'first' and 'second' urbanization in Sri Lanka: a review". 1987. Paper

Bandaranayake, Senake, and Gamini Jayasinghe. The Rock and Wall Paintings of Sri Lanka. Colombo: Lake House hop, 1986. Print.

Bandaranayake, Senake. Sigiriya: City, Palace, and Royal Gardens. Colombo: Central Cultural Fund, Ministry of Cultural Affairs, 1999. Print.

Bandaranayake, Senake. Sigiriya: City, Palace, Gardens, Monasteries, Paintings. Colombo: Central Cultural Fund, 2005. Print

Bandaranayake, Senake. Sinhalese Monastic Architecture: The Viharas of Anuradhapura. Leiden: Brill, 1974. Print.

Bandaranayake, Senake. "Amongst Asia's Earliest Surviving Gardens: The Royal and Monastic Gardens of Sigiriya and Anuradhapura." 3-36.

Bandaranayake, Senake. "6 The Lion Mountain and the Palace in the Sky Notes on the Identity of the Royal Complex at Sigiriya." Abhinandanamala: Nandana Chutiwongs Felicitation Volume : Supplementum. By P. L. Prematilleke. Bangkok: Abhinandanamala Committee, 2010. 110-37. Print.

Bandaranayake, Senake. "Sigiriya." The Cultural Triangle of Sri Lanka. Paris: UNESCO Pub., 1993. 112-35. Print.

Bendall, Cecil. "Turnour, George." Def. DNB00. Dictionary of National Biography, 1885-1900. Vol. 57. N.p.: n.p., n.d. Print.

Bogahawatte, V. T. "Building Material of Sri Lanka." Science Education Series 32 (1993): n. pag. Print.

Carotenuto, Gianna. "Domesticating the Harem." UCLA Center for India and South Asia ::. N.p., May 2008. Web. 01 Sept. 2012.

Cave, Henry William. The Ruined Cities of Ceylon: Illustrated with Photographs Taken by the Author in the Year 1896. London: Hutchinson &, 1907. Print.

Cengage., Gale. "5th Century A.D." Enotes.com. Enotes.com, 2006. Web. 02 June 2012.

Chandrasekera, M. S., E. R. Wikramanayak. "Skeletal Finds at Cobra Hood Cave, Sigiriya - A Preliminary Study." The Ceylon Journal of Medical Science (1992 Charles, Walker. Wonders of the Ancient World. London: Orbis, 1980. Print.

Coulardeau, Jacques. "'A Buddhist Debate in the Sigiri Graffiti' by Jacques Coulardeau." 'A Buddhist Debate in the Sigiri Graffiti' by Jacques Coulardeau. Open Access Essays, 13 June 2010. Web. 25 June 2012.

Dharmadasa, K. N. "The Untenability of the Tara Theory." The Island-Saturday Magazine. N.p., n.d. Web. 04 Oct. 2012.

Davids, Rhys T.W. "Sigiri, the Lion Rock, near Pulastipura, Ceylon; and the Thirty-ninth Chapter of the Mahavamsa." Journal of the Royal Asiatic Society ns VII (1875): 191-220. Print

De Alwis, Malathi. "Sexuality in the Field of Vision - The Discursive Clothing of The Sigiriya Frescoes." Embodied Violence: Communalising Female Sexuality in South Asia. London: Zed, 1996. 89-112. Print.

De Silva, Nimal, and Shabna Cader. "The Decorative Art Tradition in Ola Leaf Manuscripts." Lecture

De Silva, Nimal. "Sigiriya, Mirror Wall & Graffiti." National Trust Sri Lanka Public Lecture. Colombo. 29 June 2012. Lecture.

De Silva, P.L.N. "The Sigiriya Story, DhammaWeb News." Asian Tribune, 24 Nov. 2006. Web. 09 June 2012.

De, Silva R. H. Sigiriya and Its Significance: A Mahayana-Theravada Buddhist Monastery. Nawala: Bibliotheque, 2002. Print

De Silva, R. H. "Book Review Siri Gunasinghe's Sigiriya, Kassapa's Homage to Beauty." The Island-Saturday Magazine. N.p., n.d. Web. 20 Aug. 2012.

Dhammakitti, Louis Corneille Vijayasimha, George Turnour, and Mahanama. The Mahavansa, Part II. Containing Chapters XXXIX. . Colombo: H.M. Richards, Acting Government Printer, Ceylon, 1909. Print

Dhammika, K. "Sacred Island - A Buddhist Pilgrim's Guide to Sri Lanka." BuddhaNet 2007. Web. 30 Sept. 2009.

Dissanayake, Daya. "The Sigiri Rock." The Saadhu Testament. 3 Apr. 1999. Web. 03 Oct. 2009.

Ellepola, Chandana. "Sigiriya Water Gardens, and the Hydraulics of Sigiriya Complex Lecture 10." Lecture. The Irrigation Pattern of Sigiriya Region. Vol. 5. Colombo: Archaeological Department, 1990. 177-224. Print. Ser. 11.

Epasinghe, Premasara. "Fresco disaster at Sigiriya in 1967." Sri Lanka News. 1 Nov. 2003. Web. 28 Sept. 2009.

Faxian, and James Legge. A Record of Buddhist Kingdoms: Being an Account by the Chinese Monk Fa-Hien of His Travels in India and Ceylon (A.D. 399-414) in Search of the Buddhist Books of Discipline. New York: Paragon Book Reprint, 1965. Print.

Fernando, Ksiahnie S. "Sigiriya Rock Fortress." Daily Mirror, 24 May 2004. Web. 03 Oct. 2009.

Fernando, Romesh. "The Garb of Innocence: A Time of Toplessness, N.p., 15 Nov. 1992. Web. 15 Oct. 2012.

Forbes, Jonathan, and George Turnour. Eleven Years in Ceylon. Comprising Sketches of the Field Sports and Natural History of That Colony, and an Account of Its History and Antiquities. London: R. Bentley, 1841. Print

Geiger, Wilhelm. Culavamsa Being The More Recent Part Of Mahavamsa 2 Vols. 1998. Print. First Published in 1929.

Gunasinghe, Siri. Sigiriya: Kassapa's Homage to Beauty. Colombo: Vijitha Yapa Publications, 2008. Print.

Guruge, Ananda W. "Senarat Paranavitana as a Writer of Historic Fiction in Sanskrit." Vidyodaya J. Soc 7.1 & 2 (1996): 157-79. Print

Harischandra, Walisinha. The Scared City of Anuradhapura. New Delhi: Asian Educational Services, 1998. Print.

Indicopleustes, Comas. "CH XI - A Description of Indian Animals, and of the Island of Taprobane." Christian Topography. 550AD. 358-73. Print.

James, Tennent E. Ceylon. An Account of the Island, Physical, Historical, and Topographical with Notices of Its Natural History, Antiquities and Productions. London: Longman, Green, Longman and Roberts, 1860. The Project Gutenberg EBook. Web. 26 May 2012.

Jones-Bateman, Dorothy. "Sigiriya: The Lion Rock.". An Illustrated Guide to the Buried Cities of Ceylon. Madras: Asian Educational Services, 1994. Print.

Karunaratne, L. K. "The History of Buddhist Architecture in Sri Lanka." Digital Library & Museum of Buddhist Studies. N.p., 1998. Web. 4 Aug. 2012.

Kumar,, D. Udaya, G. V. V, U. A. Athvankar. "Traditional Writing System in Southern India Palm Leaf Manuscripts." Design Thoughts (2009): n. pag. Print.

Lanerolle, Nalini De. A Reign of Ten Kings: Sri Lanka - the World (500 B.C.-1200 A.D.) /by Nalini De Lanerolle. Colombo}: Ceylon Tourist Board, 1990. Print.

Lokubandara, J. M. The Mystique of Sigiriya: Whispers of the Mirror Wall. Colombo: Godage International, 2007. Print.

Mahanama, Dhammakitti, Wilhelm Geiger, Ruwan Rajapakse. Concise Mahavamsa : History of Buddhism in Sri Lanka. Maplewood, NJ:, 2003. Print

Malalasekara, Narada G.P., and K. Wimalajothi. Buddhism Cluture & Sri Lanka Pilgrim's Guide. Dehiwela: Buddist Cultural Centre, 2008. Print.

Marasinghe E.W,. The Vastuvidya? Sastra Ascribed to Manjusri: Text Deciphered and Translated. Delhi, India: Sri Satguru Publications, 1989. Print.

Mathmaluwe, M. B. "Sigiriya Paintings:The Advent of a New Interpretation." The Island-News. The Island-News, n.d. Web. 14 Aug. 2012.

Mukherji, Parul D. "The Art of Painting in Ancient India – Chitrasutra 1- 5.-" Chitrasutra (2) Sulekha.com, 10 Sept. 2008. Web. 16 July 2012.

Nardi, Isabella. The Theory of Citrasutras in Indian Painting: A Critical Re-evaluation of Their Uses and Interpretations. London: Routledge, 2006. Print

Nayannathara, S. The World of Indian Murals & Wall Paintings. N.p.: Chillie Breeze Publications, 2009. Print.

Norton, Wilson K. "Sigiriya "A Fortress in the Sky"" The National Geographic Magazine XC.5 (1946): 665-80. Print.

Paranavitana, Senarat. Art of the Ancient Sinhalese. Colombo: Lake House Investments, 1971. Print.

Paranavitana, Senarat. Glimpses of Ceylon's Past. Colombo: Lake House, 1972. 34-41. Print.

Paranavitana, Senarat. Sigiri Graffiti; Being Sinhalese Verses of the Eighth, Ninth and Tenth Centuries,. London: Published for the Govt. of Ceylon by Oxford UP, 1956. Print.

Paranavitana, Senarat. Sinhalayo. Colombo: Lake House Investments, 1967. Print.

Paranavitana, Senarat. The Story of Sigiriya. Pannipitiya: Stamford Lake Publications, 2000. Print.

Parker H., Ancient Ceylon 1909, reprinted by Asian Educational Services, New Delhi 1994

Parker, Percy L. "The Most Remarkable Fortress in the World. Some Adventures in Scaling Its Walls. The Lion Rock in Ceylon." Harmsworth Magazine 1 (1899): Print

Perera, D. G. "It Was Kassapa's Palace, Not a Monastery." Plus. Sunday Times, n.d. Web. 14 June 2012.

Perera, H. R. Buddhism in Sri Lanka: A Short History. Kandy, Sri Lanka: Buddhist Publication Society, 1988. Print.

Priyanka, Benille. Meaning of the Sigiriya Paintings: Based on Recent Archaeological Evidence. Colombo: Godage International, 2005. Print.

Ring, Trudy, Robert M. Salkin, Paul Schellinger, and Sharon E. La Boda. International Dictionary of Historic Places: Asia and Oceania. Chicago: Dearborn, 1996. Print.

Sah, Anupam. Palm Leaf Manuscripts of the World: Material, Technology and Conservation. Publication. Bhubaneswar: Orissa Art Conservation Centre, n.d. Print.

Schlingloff, Dieter. Narrative Wall Paintings. New Delhi: Munshiram Manoharlal Publ., 1999. Print.

Siddhartha, R. "Mahanama in the Pali Literature." The Indian Historical Quarterly 8.3 (1932): 462-65. Print.

Senaveratna, John M. Royalty in Ancient Ceylon: During the Period of the "great Dynasty" New Delhi: Asian Educational Services, 2005. Print.

Seneviratne, Sudharshan. Sigiriya Museum and Information Centre. Colombo: Publication Unit, Central Cultural Fund, 2009. Print.

Silva, K. M. De. A History of Sri Lanka. New York: Penguin Books, 2005. Print.

Sivasundaram, Sujit. Islanded: Britain, Sri Lanka, and the Bounds of an Indian Ocean Colony. New Delhi, India: Oxford UP, 2014. Print.

Solangaarachchi, Rose. "History of Metallurgy & Ancient Iron Smelting." Vidurawa (n.d.): n. pag. Rpt. in Postgraduate Institute of Archaeology. N.p.: Vidurawa, n.d. Web. 4 Aug. 2012.

Tilakaratne, Asanga. "Wondering about Sigiriya - Review of Sigiriya: Kassapa's Homage to Beauty." The Island-News. The Island-News, n.d. Web. 29 June 2012.

Traylor, Dean. "The History and Significance of the Apsaras." Helium. Helium, 03 Oct. 2010. Web. 18 July 2012.

Turnour George. The First Twenty Chapters of the Mahawanso; and a Prefatory Essay on Pali Buddhistical Literature, Originally Pub. as an Introduction to the above Mentioned Portion of the Mahawanso and to the Epitome of the History of Ceylon, and the Historical Inscriptions, Printed in the Ceylon Almanacs of 1833 and 1834:. Ceylon: Cotta Church Mission, 1836. Print

Walsh, John. "Life in the Royal Harem - The Women of Ancient India's Kings." SE Asian History. N.p., 25 Sept. 2007. Web. 01 Sept. 2012.

Wijesinghe, Pushpitha. "Ancient Ingenuity - Sigiriya Moat." Articlesbase.com. Articlesbase.com, 23 Apr. 2012. Web. 21 May 2012.

Wiley, Lucia. "The Art of Fresco: Painting Technique." The Art of Fresco: Painting Technique. N.p., n.d. Web. 15 July 2012.

Williams, Harry. Ceylon; Pearl of the East. London: Robert Hall Limited, 1963. 75-99. Print.

Woodhouse, Leslie Ann. "Comparative Harems: Women, Sex and Family Structures from the Middle East to South & Southeast Asia ."" ORIAS 2011 Summer Institute, n.d. Web. 5 Sept. 2012.

"Buddhist Beliefs about the Afterlife." Reincarnation and Afterlife in Buddhism. N.p., n.d. Web. 13 May 2013.

"Buddhist Studies: Rebirth." Buddhist Studies: Rebirth. N.p., n.d. Web. 13 May 2013.

"Climate of the Dry Zone." Dambulla Sigiriya Tourism Promotion. Association for Dambulla Sigiriya Tourism Promotion. Web. 23 May 2012.

"Figurines Excavated from Sigiriya." Lanka Library Forum. LANKALIBRARY FORUM, 4 Mar. 2006. Web. 12 May 2012.

"Glossary of Buddhism." - ReligionFacts. N.p., n.d. Web. 13 May 2013.

"History - Sigiriya - Lion Rock Citadel." History - Sigiriya - Lion Rock Citadel. N.p., n.d. Web. 08 July 2012.

"Organisation of the Ancient Sri Lanka Armies. Â« Ancient Sri Lankan Coins." Ancient Sri Lankan Coins. N.p., n.d. Web. 29 Sept. 2012.

"Shekhawati Festival." Shekhawati Festival. N.p., n.d. Web. 14 July 2012.

"Sigiri Graffiti: poetry on the mirror-wall." Web. 30 Sept. 2009.

"Shuttleworth Collection: Archaeological Views of Sri Lanka and Southern India." The British Library. N.p., n.d. Web. 20 June 2012.

The Cultural Triangle of Sri Lanka. [Paris]: UNESCO Pub., 2004. Print.

"The Mahavamsa." Wisdom Library. N.p., n.d. Web. 04 July 2012.

"Transmigration Of Souls - A Buddhist Perspective." Transmigration Of Souls From A Buddhist Perspective. N.p., n.d. Web. 13 May 2013

Photographs

The photographs and illustrations used in this book are by the author with the exception of those cited below.

Terraced Wall with Brick Cladding Contents Page – Sandie Mumme, Buddha Statue Dambulla Temple – Paul Mannix, Kala Wewa - Badra Kamaladasa, Ivory Carving of a King and Entourage Mounted on a War Elephant – Bayerische Schlösserverwlatung www.residenz-muenchen.de, Fresco Montages – Sandie Mumme, Elephant Carrying a Log – Skeen & Co www.imagesofceylon.com, Ancient Bullock Cart Ceramic Figure - www.dollsofindia.com, Men Carrying Baskets - Frederic Courtland Penfield www.gutenberg.org, Elephant Hitched to a Cart – Skeen & Co www.imagesofceylon.com, Women laborers carrying bricks at a construction site – dpirhana, Sigiriya Rock at Sunset – Roger Sargent, Mr. Perera on Scaffolding – Skeen & Co www.imagesofceylon.com, Stairway to Sigiriya Rock Fortress, Sri Lanka 1895. National Library of Australia. Photograph. Album of the Boileau Family's Voyage from England to Australia in 1894-1895., Canberra. , Lotus in pond on summit – Mathieu Castel, Inner Moat – Makiwo Chew, Fountain Gardens Meandering Stream – Sandie Mumme, Fountain Gardens Pond with Waterfalls - Giorgio Bassetti, Mirror Wall Steps – Yvonne M. de la Cuesta, Frescoes – Red Clouds – David Alexander Elder, Spiral Staircase from below – Ahmad Saifuddin Abdullah , Sigiriya Summit Arial – Amila Tennakoon, Bamboo Scaffolding – Lorna, Wood Apple Fruit – Wikipedia, Stone Fruit – Wikipedia.

INDEX

The Sigiriya Earring is made of solid gold but is extremely light-weight. The goldsmith used a hollow-core technique to keep weight to a minimum. Twirling scroll-like vortices are repeated on the front and back of the earring. At the center of the vortices is a milky white quartz stone, its twin on the back has been lost. Hanging from the pendant are three semi-precious gems. The earring does not bear any resemblance to those depicted in the frescoes, suggesting that it probably isn't from the time of Kasyapa. It probably belongs to a period between the 8th and 10th centuries. How the earring ended up at Sigiriya is uncertain. Some suggest that it may have been lost by a rich patron or tourist while visiting the site. Others suggest that it was gifted to the monastery. Who knows; it may even have belonged to a woman of King Kasyapa's harem. We will never know.

www.ingramcontent.com/pod-product-compliance
Lightning Source LLC
LaVergne TN
LVHW070212110826
845147LV00003B/564

* 9 7 8 0 9 8 7 3 4 5 1 7 2 *